Animals of Europe
the ecology of the wildlife

Typically, the European robin makes its nest in a hole in a bank, but it is a great opportunist so far as nesting sites are concerned. Robins not uncommonly nest in odd places, in a tin can thrown into a hedge, in an old boot or in any artificial cavity of this sort.

Animals of Europe
the ecology of the wildlife
by Maurice Burton

Holt, Rinehart & Winston
NEW YORK, CHICAGO, SAN FRANCISCO

Library of Congress Catalog Card Number: 73-7171

Library of Congress Cataloging in Publication Data

Burton, Maurice, 1898–
    Animals of Europe.

    SUMMARY: An account of man's impact on the
ecology of Europe describing the adjustment of
various animal species to human intrusion.
        1. Zoology–Europe–Ecology–Juvenile literature.
2. Zoology–Europe–Juvenile literature.
[1. Zoology–Europe. 2. Ecology–Europe.]
I. Title.
QL253.B87 1973   591.9'4   73-7171
ISBN 0-03-011181-1

Printed in the Netherlands by Smeets Offset, Weert
First American edition

The European bison lived throughout the deciduous forests of
Europe, including Sweden, but excluding the British Isles, until
the sixteenth century. It became extinct in the wild in the 1920s
but a herd collected from individuals in parks and zoos has been
liberated in the Bielowecza forest in Poland and is now thriving.

Index compiled by Jacqueline Pinhey

Copyright © 1973 by Eurobook Limited

Published simultaneously in Canada by
Holt, Rinehart and Winston of Canada, Limited

Library of Congress Catalog Card Number: 73-7171

Library of Congress Cataloging in Publication Data

Burton, Maurice, 1898–
    Animals of Europe.

    SUMMARY: An account of man's impact on the
ecology of Europe describing the adjustment of
various animal species to human intrusion.
        1. Zoology–Europe–Ecology–Juvenile literature.
2. Zoology–Europe–Juvenile literature.
[1. Zoology–Europe. 2. Ecology–Europe.]
I. Title.
QL253.B87 1973   591.9'4   73-7171
ISBN 0-03-011181-1

Printed in the Netherlands by Smeets Offset, Weert
First American edition

The European bison lived throughout the deciduous forests of
Europe, including Sweden, but excluding the British Isles, until
the sixteenth century. It became extinct in the wild in the 1920s
but a herd collected from individuals in parks and zoos has been
liberated in the Bielowecza forest in Poland and is now thriving.

Animals of Europe
the ecology of the wildlife
by Maurice Burton

Holt, Rinehart & Winston
NEW YORK, CHICAGO, SAN FRANCISCO

Introduction

According to the *Iliad* there are two versions as to the identity of Europa. One has it that she was the daughter of Phoenix. The other, based on common tradition, identifies her as the daughter of the Phoenician king Agenor. When Europa and her maidens were playing on the seashore they were visited by Zeus in the form of a bull. Europa playfully climbed on to his back whereupon Zeus rushed into the sea and swam with her to the island of Crete. There she bore Minos, Rhadamanthus and Sarpedon, all sired by Zeus. Later, so the story goes, she married Asterion, king of Crete.

How and when her name came to be given to a continent is obscure. It is sufficient to know that Europa became eventually the name of one of the three divisions of the then known world, the other two being Asia and Africa. Used as a territorial name, Europa first appears in the Homeric *Hymn to Apollo*, applied to the mainland of Hellas, but excluding Peloponnesus and the neighbouring islands. Aeschylus and Heredotus first used it as one of the divisions of the world known to the ancient Greeks. Asia, the second of the three divisions, was at first used for the western end of what is now Asia Minor. Africa was used in two senses: one for that part of the continent known to the ancients; the other more restricted and applied only to the region better known as Carthage.

In due course, the name Europe was given to the whole of the eastern end of the vast land mass sometimes referred to as Eurasia. It includes also the large and somewhat distant island of Iceland, which will be largely ignored in the narrative which follows. This is not to belittle the importance of Iceland, but more because its inclusion in Europe is politically arbitrary and also because most of the island lies within the Arctic proper, the subject of Bernard Stonehouse's companion book in this series.

Political Europe, as now understood, lies for the most part within the cool temperate zone. It almost escapes any part of it lying within the Arctic proper (see p. 21) and the warmest, southernmost parts lie well north of the tropics. The warm waters of the North Atlantic Drift— commonly referred to as the Gulf Stream— bring warm air to much of western Europe in winter, so that Europe as a whole is less cold than other lands in the same latitudes. As a result, there are few places in Europe where it is too cold in winter or too hot in summer to work out-of-doors. This fact alone must have had a tremendous influence on the agriculture, the industries, even on the arts and sciences of Europe, and with them the growth of what is now generally called, perhaps not without its touch of arrogance, western civilization. Another factor that is probably not without its importance is that in few other parts of the world is there such a varied topography and scenery. This is reflected more especially in the variety of mammals, which are relatively diverse compared with the small area of land concerned.

The peoples inhabiting the continent of Europe are as varied as its scenery, but for entirely different reasons. They are the product of repeated waves of migration, colonization and invasion, which alone suggests that this corner of the Afro-Eurasian land mass has always been attractive to the peoples who colonized Europe from the south and more especially from the east. European history since the fall of the Roman Empire has seen a succession of invaders pouring through the steppes corridor from central and south-west Asia to southern Russia. As the Ice Age ended there began a migration into Europe along the same route, especially by mammals. Or it might be more correct to say that the mammal invaders are more obvious, largely on account of their size.

What follows here is mainly an outline sketch of the European fauna today. An attempt is made also to picture the animals of Europe as Stone Age men must have known them and to compare this with the position as it is today.

Maurice Burton

11

birch wood

bison

mammoth

pine marten

red squirrel

roe deer

cots pine

The European Region

alder

whitebeam

oak

ash

elk

Cro-Magnon man

brown bear

lynx

beaver

tarpan

History of settlement

According to the theory of continental drift, around 400 million years ago the land surface of our planet formed one continuous mass. The rest was water. This one mass, roughly circular with its centre about where the Sahara now is, began to fragment a hundred million years ago. To the south a lump moved away, later to split again to form the continents of Australia and Antarctica. The north-east mass slewed away to form Asia. To the west the continent of America began its slow journey into isolation. Africa all but severed its connexion, so that it was joined to Asia only by the the Isthmus of Suez (subsequently severed by the building of the Suez Canal). To the west of the vast land mass now called Asia there was considerable fragmentation, to give the continent of Europe.

The relentless movements in the earth's outer skin that tore the original land mass apart and scattered the separate parts asunder tore a gap between southern Europe and North Africa, letting in the sea to form the Mediterranean and Black Seas. At the same time corrugations were formed on the northern side to raise the mountains of Iberia, Switzerland and the Balkans, the reverberations of which still echo from time to time in earthquakes and volcanic eruptions. In the north of what is now called Europe, another series of natural phenomena caused a rent, now filled by the Baltic, and threw up the mountains forming the spine of Scandinavia. In between was left the vast flat expanse of land of the North European Plain, extending from western and northern France, through northern Germany and Poland to embrace almost all of European Russia as far as the Urals, as well as Finland.

The broken outline of Europe, with nearly 50,000 miles of coastline, means that few centres of human population today are more than 500 miles from a port. This has had a profound effect on the course of human history. It has led to the exploitation of the sea, both for its natural resources, especially in fisheries, and to the use of water as a means of transport, as a cheap and easy way of carrying goods from one part to another. The stimulus it gave to the building of ships and encouraging breeds of seafarers resulted in the European expansion to all corners of the earth.

When man first began to colonize Europe is as yet uncertain, as is his place of origin. Paleolithic or Old Stone Age man was in occupation over 600,000 years ago. To begin with his stone implements were large nodules or flakes of stone crudely shaped by coarse chipping into rough hand axes. As time passed he perfected his skill, producing recognizable scrapers, borers and knives. He probably used wooden implements and he may have used bone, horn and antler, but if so these have decayed, leaving only his stone implements to bear witness to his former presence here. The first evidence we have of the people themselves is a lower jaw bone, from Mauer, near Heidelberg, in Germany, not much less than 500,000 years old. The jaw is massive and lacks a chin eminence, one of the distinctions between the ape and man. The next is from Swanscombe, in Kent, in south-east England, part of a skull and two large bones 250,000 years old, in the middle of the second interglacial period. The next positive remains were from Steinheim, in Germany, probably 150,000 years old, roughly in the middle of the third interglacial period. They show the heavy-browed condition normally associated in the popular mind with prehistoric man, but the skull as a whole shows some resemblances to that of modern man.

These representatives of the very early inhabitants of Europe are less familiar than Neanderthal man. From 1848 onwards have been found the remains of nearly 40 individuals, from the Neanderthal Valley, near Düsseldorf, in Germany, Belgium, the Channel Islands, south-west France, Gibraltar, Italy, Croatia, North Africa, Palestine, southern Russia and Siberia. Neanderthal man was less erect than modern man, not so tall, and his skull shows heavy brow ridges, a sloping forehead and a lower jaw lacking a chin eminence. These remains are associated with worked flint implements, of the type known as Mousterian, and in one instance there is evidence of ceremonial burial. This was at La-Chapelle-aux-Saints, in France. The body had been buried in a contracted position, in a hollow in the cave floor, together with numerous broken bones and flint implements. The bones were mainly of bison, reindeer and woolly rhinoceros, and one leg bone of a bison showed that it must have been buried with flesh still on it. From all this it is reasonable to suppose that the corpse had been buried with food intended for the departed spirit. More important, the burial contains one of the many clues that help in tracing the move-

Previous page: Most of the animals in this artist's impression of a scene in prehistoric Europe survive today, some in restricted numbers. Two are extinct: the tarpan or wild horse and the woolly mammoth.

The theory of continental drift: the four maps show the probabl course of the evolution of continents.

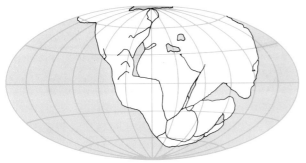

1 Continuous land mass that existed up to 150 million years ago.

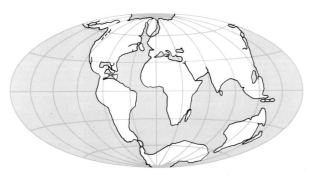

2 In Mesozoic times, 120 million years ago, the Americas are moving westwards and Australasia and Antarctica are moving southwards and to the east.

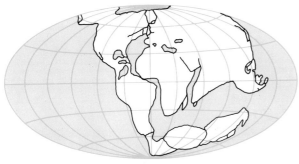

3 In the early Tertiary, 60 million years ago, the continents are beginning to take up their present positions.

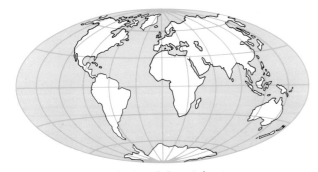

4 The present-day distribution of the continents.

Table showing the probable relationships of Paleolithic cultures in Europe to the glacial periods (ice ages) and interglacial periods, with an estimated time scale. *(After F. E. Zeurer and W. E. Le Gros Clark)*

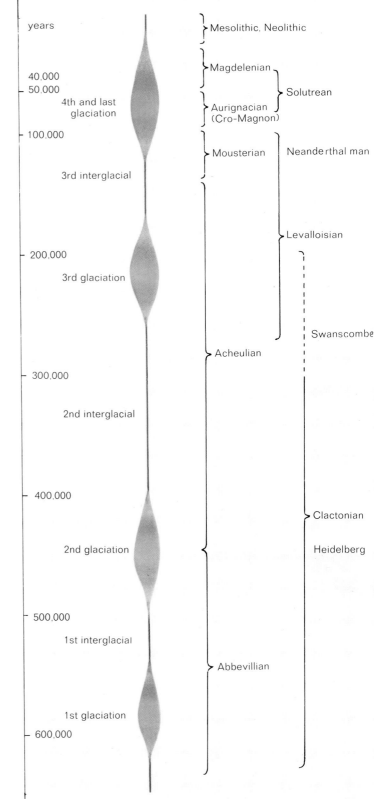

years

40,000
50,000
4th and last glaciation

Mesolithic, Neolithic

Magdelenian

Solutrean

Aurignacian (Cro-Magnon)

100,000

Mousterian — Neanderthal man

3rd interglacial

Levalloisian

200,000

3rd glaciation

Swanscombe

300,000

2nd interglacial

Acheulian

400,000

2nd glaciation

Clactonian

Heidelberg

500,000

1st interglacial

Abbevillian

1st glaciation

600,000

15

ments of animals in the Europe of those times.

Neanderthal man appears to have died out in Europe about 40,000 years ago. He was succeeded by Cro-Magnon man or, as he is usually now called, Aurignacian man. It has been suggested that Aurignacian man probably migrated to Europe from Asia, possibly through the steppes corridor. The remains found at Cro-Magnon, in France, indicate a tall, muscular race, with a brain equal to that of the modern European, and facial features not unlike those found in some parts of Europe today. The Cro-Magnon were responsible for the finest of the cave-paintings in France. They had long narrow skulls and short broad faces. Their paintings of reindeer, bison and other animals furnish more clues to the contemporary fauna.

In some parts of Europe the Aurignacian culture was followed by the Solutrean, which was of short duration and was succeeded by the Magdalenian. This was during the last half of the final Ice Age, when the climate of Europe was positively arctic and the reindeer was abundant in southern Europe. The few human remains of this period so far found suggest that the Magdalenians had Eskimo-like features, and it has been suggested that as the ice-cap receded, at the end of the Ice Age, they moved north, following the migrating reindeer. This is a reasonable theory although it requires substantiation.

The Magdalenian period lasted from 20,000 years ago to 10,000, to a time when the melting ice caused a rise in the sea-level which cut off the British Isles from the rest of Europe and flooded the Baltic basin, as well as producing other changes in

Europe's outline. It ushered in the Mesolithic period, or Middle Stone Age, during which the huge stone circles were erected, giving the most solid evidence we have of the birth of a religion. The Mesolithic and Neolithic (New Stone Age) periods together covered a span of some 10,000 years and, with the Bronze Age which followed, carried Europe into the Iron Age, with its eventual industrial revolutions and the nuclear age.

Throughout the Stone Ages people must have lived in small isolated groups, as the African Bushmen and the Australian Aborigines do today.

Left: Glaciers help us to visualize what much of Europe must have looked like during the successive Ice Ages that preceded man's colonization of the continent.

A silver birch woodland in winter presents a picture that has been recurring annually for thousands of years since the great ice cap receded and left Europe habitable.

Probably a community of 500 was exceptional and 50–100 the more usual. That they had little contact with one another is seen in their distinct tool-making techniques. They were hunters and food-gatherers, making use of available natural resources, therefore needing to preserve each its territory, much as troops of monkeys do. If members of these communities met at all it would have been only at the boundaries of their territories and they would at most have made faces and threatening gestures at each other.

Sexual dimorphism, that is differences between the sexes, was more pronounced than today, especially in stature, the women being markedly smaller than the men. At the same time, isolated communities give the best opportunities for mutations to arise, so that each community would tend

BRUEMMER

Prehistoric man lived with the reindeer in southern Europe while the ice cap persisted and migrated north with it as the climate grew less severe. Until recent times the domesticated reindeer supplied almost all the needs of the Lapps of northern Europe.

Bracken regenerating through burnt gorse. The conversion of the primeval forests to agricultural land was a slow and painstaking process in which fire played an important part.

Fire is still used to a limited extent in agriculture, though in recent years the practice of burning unwanted stubble after the harvest has become more common.

HAWKES/NHPA

GOODERS/ARDEA

18

to develop its peculiar characteristics. Therefore while we may speak of Neanderthal man ranging from Gibraltar to Siberia, as if it were a homogeneous race, the differences from one area to another, in physique and culture, would have been as great, or greater, than those between the tribes of Africa before the European infiltration.

As the last of the Ice Ages drew to a close, and changes in the vegetation and the animals increased with the warmer climate, there would be corresponding changes in the human inhabitants. One result probably was a greater freedom of movement and an increased rate of survival and therefore growth in the populations. This would have resulted in more inter-mingling, with greater interbreeding, accompanied by major spreading of some sub-races at the expense of others. The sub-race known as the Mediterranean Proper, for example, is known to have spread from the Mesolithic Natufians of Palestine along both northern and southern shores of the Mediterranean. They were preceded by the Early Mediterranean, of which the Basques, peculiar in their blood grouping and language, are the sole remaining remnant of the early Neolithic population of Europe.

The gipsies are also Mediterranean Proper, but they came from northern India, and since they and other races colonized Europe from south-west Asia it is reasonable that some animals also followed this route.

The earliest known traces of Neolithic man are from Jericho and are dated 7000 B.C. By 3000 B.C. at the latest, the first agriculturalists and herdsmen had spread into Europe from what is now called the Middle East. They mixed with hunters already there. The supply of food became more stable, populations increased. Man's impact on his environment was beginning to show the effects so familiar in this modern age. Land would be cleared of forest for crops, dispossessing animals of their habitat but allowing some to become parasitic on stored foods. The agriculturalists spread along both shores of the Mediterranean and also northwards over the fertile soil of the Danube Valley. In northern Europe, however, the hunting communities still continued, with reindeer-herding and fishing as the basis of existence, much as in the extreme north of Europe today.

The Bronze Age began in the Middle East about 4000 B.C. and continued for 1,500 years, until displaced by the Iron Age. It spread late into Europe but there it lasted only 600 years. Never-

theless, it promoted trade, bronze objects being exchanged for local products. Trade routes began to be opened up and marriages between peoples of distant races resulted in increasing mixtures of bloods. Meanwhile, the climate was becoming drier so that in places forests were being replaced by open scrub and grasslands. This was reinforced by the burn-and-till type of agriculture. Together, they made more room for expanding human populations and encouraged pastoral nomadism. Concurrently, merchants from the eastern Mediterranean were following the sea route taken by the Neolithic megalith builders to Spain, France, Britain and Scandinavia.

It was a period of expansion in Europe but because cremation was so widely practised during the Bronze Age, the details of the spread and mixing of the races are to a large extent permanently obscured. What is certain is that bronze weapons made conquest easy, and with the coming of the Iron Age and more superior weapons the pace of conquest increased. So also did the hunters' ability to kill large animals. The Bronze Age culture spread earlier into Asia than into Europe, as did the Iron Age culture. During the early Iron Age, barbarians from Asia overran eastern and central Europe and the fringes of the Mediterranean area. Among these were the Celts, the survivors of whom are today found in Brittany, Wales, Scotland and western Ireland. The overthrow of the Classical Mediterranean civilizations was complete by A.D. 500 and during the next thousand years there were successive invasions by Mongols into eastern and central Europe.

During the Bronze Age, and more particularly the Iron Ages, village settlements grew into towns. These concentrations of people caused an increase in infections. They also affected the fashions in feeding, leading away from the more natural, balanced diets and giving rise to the spread of nutritional deficiencies. Other factors began to affect the physique. In an urban way of life strength and endurance become less important. There is a division of labour within the town's inhabitants and also between the town-dweller and village-dweller. The day of classes and castes had arrived, and with it the birth of sedentary occupations, intellectuals, more leisure and more attention to the arts. The seeds of industrial unrest, class warfare and the other ills that afflict Europe today had their seeds in the Bronze and Iron Ages. The more settled way of life gave greater opportunities for domestication of animals. With the growth of a leisured class there must have been an incentive to keep pets.

These two Ages also determined the present peoples of Europe and to a large extent the kaleidoscope of nations that make up political Europe. The mixture of peoples is such that no comprehensive name for them is truly satisfactory. In everyday speech they are referred to as Whites, although they include many with dark skins, the darkest being darker than the lightest of the so-called black races. The term "European" is unsatisfactory because the European populations include those of North African and Asian descent, as indeed do the populations of animals. So it has become the practice among anthropologists, in grouping the members of the human species, to speak of them as Caucasoids, so demarcating them from the Mongoloids, Negroids and Australoids (including Pacific Islanders) who represent the other three groups.

The name "Caucasoid" was first used in the late eighteenth century by J. F. Blumenbach to denote the peoples of the Caucasus, which he was then studying. Since this region probably represents the point of origin for a substantial proportion of the peoples of Europe today the name has been adopted for the whole, as a matter of convenience.

More human history has been made in Europe than in any other continent despite the fact that civilizations in Asia and Egypt preceded those of Greece and Rome by several thousand years. Europe is less than a quarter the size of Asia and would probably have been considered as part of the larger continent had there not existed a natural boundary formed by the Ural Mountains, the Caspian Sea, the Caucasus Mountains and the Black Sea and Sea of Marmora. Another factor has been the dramatic outstripping of the rest of the world, formerly, in industry and commerce.

The reasons for this outstripping are manifold. To begin with, Europe has no appreciable desert areas, so a greater proportion of the land could be farmed than in any other continent. Its ragged outline makes the sea more readily accessible to a

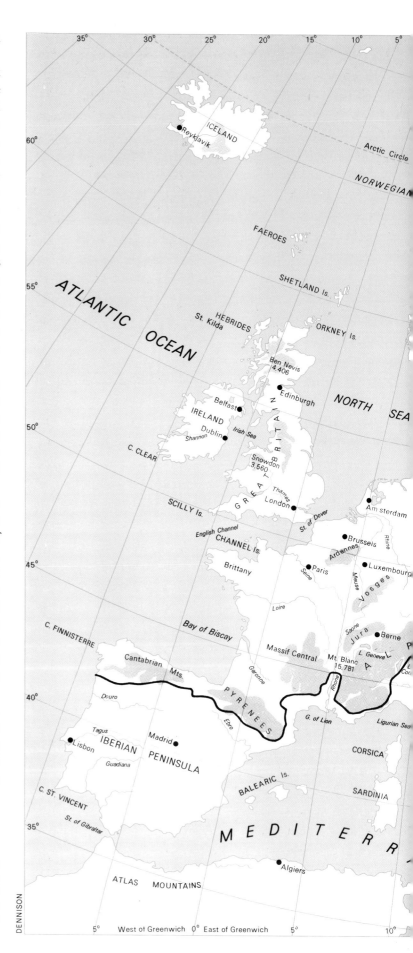

Map of Europe showing the vegetation zones and the principal cities, rivers and mountain ranges. Climatically, Europe can be divided into four main regions: subarctic, continental, atlantic and mediterranean. Politically it stretches from Norway in the north to the Mediterranean in the south; eastwards into Russia as far as the Urals, and west to include the distant island of Iceland.

20

NORTH CAPE

LAPLAND

L. Inari

West Siberian Plain

Kanin Peninsula

Pechora

U R A L S

Teloos Iz 5,305

60°

SEA

Kebnekaise 6,965

Imandra Oz

Kola Peninsula

WHITE SEA

N. Dvina

55°

Galdhopiggen 8,097

GULF OF BOTHNIA

FINLAND

L. Onega

Lake Ladoga

Rybinsk Res.

Kama

Oslo

Helsinki

ALAND Is.

Stockholm

Gulf of Finland

L. Maralen

Rybinsk Res.

Volga

Kama

L. Vanern

L. Vattern

GOTLAND

E U R O P E A N   P L A I N

Valdai Hills

CENTRAL

Oka

Volga

Obshchi Syrt

50°

Skagerrak

Jutland

Copenhagen

BALTIC SEA

N O R T H

Moscow

RUSSIAN

Volga Heights

Ural

Elbe

Berlin

Vistula

Warsaw

Pripyat

UPLANDS

Oder

PRIPYAT MARSHES

Weser

Forest

Ore Mts

Prague

Pripyat

U k r a i n e

Dnepr

Don

Volga

45°

Bohemian Forest

Moravian Hts.

C A R P A T H I A N S

Dnester

Constance

Inn

Vienna

Danube

L. Balaton Bakony Forest

Budapest

Plain of Hungary

Dnester

Odessa

Sea of Azov

CASPIAN

Garda

Po

DINARIC ALPS

Drava

Sava

Tisza

Transylvanian Alps

Prut

Crimea

CAUCASUS

Elbrus 18,481

SEA

40°

ADRIATIC

Belgrade

Bucharest

Danube

APENNINES

SEA

Sofia

B L A C K   S E A

Kura

Tiber

Rome

Balkan Peninsula

Istanbul

Ararat 16,916

Tirana

Sea of Marmara

Ankara

L. Van

TYRRHENIAN SEA

IONIAN SEA

AEGEAN SEA

A N A T O L I A

L. Tuz

Calabria

Ionian Is.

Natural Vegetation

SICILY

Athens

Morea

Taurus Mts.

South Limit of Tundra
North Limit of Coniferous Forest
North Limit of Broad-leaved Forest and Meadow
Areas of Temperate Grassland
North Limit of Mediterranean Evergreen and Shrubs

NEAN

C. MATAPAN

RHODES

CYPRUS

Scale 1:17,500,000

Malta

15°

20°

CRETE

25°

30°

35°

100 0   200   400   600 Km.

SEA

higher proportion of its inhabitants than in any other continent. It so happens that the greatest concentration of food fishes is in the northern hemisphere and especially in the North Atlantic. As we shall see later, food fisheries not only brought in great wealth and boosted the growth of commerce, during the days of the Hanseatic League, but turned villages into towns, accelerated the growth of merchant fleets and navies, and stimulated colonization, notably in North America.

Geography

Europe is rich in natural resources on and in the land. Despite deforestation it still has its fair share of timber forests. It has large deposits of coal and iron and a not inconsiderable amount of oil. Over most of the continent the climate is mild. Its mountain ranges rarely present barriers between one region and another.

Within this general picture the continent can be roughly divided into two parts, eastern and western. In the east are wide open plains seldom rising above 400 metres, stretching from the Arctic to the Black Sea, with the climate and type of country changing only gradually from one area to another. This is the area which was overrun by successive waves of invaders from Asia, using the convenient gap south of the Urals, the steppes corridor. These invasions led to the formation of the Russian Empire.

The western half of Europe contrasts sharply with the eastern half. The climate is milder and more damp than in the east. Eastern Europe is a vast plain, and although this thrusts a broad finger through northern Germany, the Low Countries and into France, continuing into the lowlands of England, and thrusting southwards along the Danube basin into the plains of Hungary, roughly south and north of this main plain are mountain ranges. So everywhere in western Europe there is quick change from lowland to mountain, from deep valley to high moorland. In this varied terrain, farm labourers, miners, artisans and factory workers and, near the ever-present coasts, fishermen, are close neighbours, supplementing and complementing each other's activities and learning from one another.

When Paleolithic man first settled in it, most of Europe would have been covered with mixed forests of evergreen trees and broad-leaved (deciduous) trees such as oak, beech and chestnut, probably with pines in the north. The movements of the ice cap during successive Ice Ages would have brought corresponding changes in the vegetation, but after the last Ice Age the vegetation would have eventually settled down to what it is today. That is, to the north the tundra, with no trees, only dwarf birches and willows, with lichen, moss and heather; south of this the taiga, with forests of pine, spruce, fir and larch; then mixed forest with broad-leaved trees.

Much of the broad-leaved forest was then destroyed for farming land, in which cereals would have become the main crops. The hardy rye was grown in the north and east, and wheat in the west and south, while barley and oats would have been grown everywhere. The wetter regions of the west allowed grass pastureland to be developed, on which dairy cattle could flourish, and later sugar beet and potatoes were added. So Europe became a major food-producing continent although today, because of its large human populations, it must import food, especially cereals and meat.

On the basis of climate four climatic regions can be recognized: subarctic, continental, atlantic and mediterranean regions. The modern method is to base the southern limits of both arctic and subarctic regions on isotherms (lines of same mean annual temperature) so ignoring the traditional line of the Arctic Circle. If the 10°C isotherm is

22

used, only the extreme northern fringes of Norway and Sweden, part of the Kola Peninsula and slightly more extensive tracts of northernmost European Russia are included in the Arctic Circle. This is the tundra where the vegetation consists of lichens, mosses and dwarf stunted trees. The southern boundary of the tundra approximates to the tree-line, and south of it is the taiga or "forest tundra" with summers too short for most crops to grow except barley and oats, potatoes and fodder hay. As a result, there are wide stretches of almost useless land, unfit for cultivation and where no one lives. The taiga takes in much of Norway, most of Sweden north of Stockholm, almost the whole of Finland and a large part of northern European U.S.S.R., as far south as Leningrad and somewhat farther south along a line from there to the Urals. In Finland, for example, much of this is rocky and bare of soil. Consequently, Finland, Sweden and Norway, which are together four times the size of the British Isles, have only a quarter as many people. Finland has few natural resources other than timber. Sweden has mineral ores and water-power from its rivers. Norway has turned to the sea, for cod and herring fisheries and whaling. The northern part of European U.S.S.R. has rich coalfields around Vortuka. In its extreme north the sparse populations rely on fishing and hunting and on the reindeer. South of this stretch vast forests of fir, spruce and larch, timber from which is exported through Archangel. Even if these were cut down, summers would be too short for profitable farming.

The region of continental climate includes the rest of European Russia and adjacent territories over most of which there are bitterly cold winters with little rain, the bulk of which falls mainly in summer. Over most of this there is only a seven-month growing period for plants, including crops, because although snow does not lie deep it persists for a long time. Typically in this area, as great as the rest of Europe, the climate becomes milder towards the south, but even in the most southerly

Left: Gulls follow a fishing boat. Europe's broken outline has meant a close association between the sea's resources and the human inhabitants of that continent, whose commerce has in the past been largely based on the herring.

A tundra scene on Varanger peninsula, northern Norway, showing scattered boulders with lichen and moss stretching away into the distance. Lichens and mosses provide valuable food for tundra-living animals.

NORSTRÖM/N

Scots pines, widely spaced on the sandy soil of the northern taiga, the forested zone of coniferous trees stretching from the Scandinavian peninsula eastwards across Europe and into Asia.

Finland in mid-winter, showing conifers in a different mood and setting, under the midnight sun. Only a few, well-adapted animals survive the winter in the far north without hibernating. These include wolves, arctic foxes and hares, wolverines, ermine and a variety of voles and lemmings.

parts, around the Black Sea, snow covers the ground for at least six weeks in the year. As the climate changes from north to south over this vast plain, with no mountain range to break it, with wide shallow river basins separated by low, wide uplands, both climate and the nature of the soil gradually change. South of the taiga lies the great triangle of mixed forest, with Moscow at its heart. It stretches from Leningrad to Kiev and the Carpathians, with its apex pointed at the southern end of the Ural Mountains. At its southern edge lies a great coalfield. South and south-east of it is the Black Earth region with a rich dark soil and few trees. This is the Ukraine, famous for its large areas of wheat, rye, barley and oats. It also includes the Donbas, the largest Russian coalfield, with rich supplies of iron ore and, nearer the Caspian Sea and north of the Caucasus, the richest oilfield in Europe. To the west lie the treeless plains of the Russian steppes.

The third main climatic region, called here the atlantic region, is sometimes called western Europe or the western lands. It is hard to define. Western Europe, logically speaking, should include the Iberian Peninsula and Italy, but both these are mediterranean in character, and "western lands" is objectionable for the same reason. The atlantic region, as a title, has the virtue, at the least, that it refers to that part of Europe where the winds blow mainly from the Atlantic Ocean, bringing most of the rain, which falls chiefly in the west of Europe; and where the warm air from the North Atlantic Drift is most strongly felt. It stretches from south-western Norway to Portugal and eastwards. In this region there is rain in every month of the year; the summers are warm rather than hot, and the winters cool rather than cold.

Eastwards the atlantic region merges into Central Europe which includes those parts lying between the southern shores of the Baltic Sea and the northern limits of the mediterranean region. It includes the German and Polish parts of the North European Plain, the plateau of southern Germany, the highest parts of the alps and the plains of Hungary. In it the climate is less equable than in the atlantic region proper and the scenery more variable than the continental region to its east. Central Europe could be considered a subdivision of the atlantic region, to which it approximates more closely than to the regions north, east or south of it.

In the atlantic region the topography is related to the North European Plain which falls gently to the coast and is continued under the sea as a broad continental shelf from which the British Isles rise like a seaward bastion. This feature alone has had an important bearing on human destinies in the region. Whereas 2,000 years or so ago it was the mediterranean region that played the major role, it was the fisheries of the shallow North Sea—alternatively called, and with sounder logic, the German Ocean—that shifted the emphasis, beginning about 500 years ago and remarkable for the rise and decline of the Hanseatic League, based on the herring fishery.

In later years the mild climate, generally damp, was ideal for dairy farming, the raising of a diversity of vegetable crops and the formation of rich pastureland for herds of beef cattle and for pigs and poultry. There was abundance of easily mined

Not all Europe was originally forest-covered. The vast plains of the Steppes probably appeared much as they do in this scene from Rumania. The ancestors of the sheep, however, were found more on the highlands, where grass and other herbage were sparse and coarse.

The fertile atlantic region of Europe. A scene in southern England with downland (South Downs) in the distance and arable land stretching from its southern slopes to the lowland in the foreground. The mild, generally damp climate of the atlantic region is ideal for both arable and dairy farming.

coal for heavy industry and the advantage of sea-ways and ports for bringing in raw materials from overseas. This is where the best breeds of sheep, cattle and pigs were originated and the best strains of vegetable crops, and where steam in industry was pioneered and developed.

France offers in effect a bridge between the atlantic region proper and the subdivision of Central Europe. Her northern and western provinces are typical of the atlantic region and she has a central plateau comparable to the German plateau, and in the east she has high mountains. Her southern provinces are mediterranean.

The fourth of our regions, the mediterranean, has hot summers almost without rain and is seldom really cold except in the mountains, which are a conspicuous feature of the region. It also has proximity to the sea, but it is a sea that lacks the abundance of food fishes available to the atlantic region. This may be why so much use is made of sea foods other than fish. On the land farming is difficult and involves terracing the slopes to obtain an adequate depth of soil, and watering because of the long dry summers. Fruit growing is the predominant husbandry, with grapes, olives, nuts and the citrus fruits outstanding. In Greece, for example,

Olive trees at Delphi, in Greece. The olive tree is small and ever-green, with narrow leaves and inconspicuous greenish-white flowers. Its stone-fruit is the olive of commerce. Cultivated varieties date from prehistoric times.

Mount Olympus, in Greece, one of the best known if not the most famous of the features of Mediterranean Europe. Its slopes bear trees and shrubs, the maquis of southern Europe.

A scene unhappily all too familiar in Europe today; the countryside in Kent, south-eastern England, scarred as a motorway is built.

less than a twentieth of the land can be tilled, and there, as in other parts of the mediterranean region, arid, scrub-covered land can only be used for somewhat poor sheep grazing.

The mediterranean region is generally poor in minerals and the dry summers mean that little water-power is available, except, for instance, on the Plain of Lombardy in Italy, where the alpine streams can be harnessed for electricity. Wheat, maize and rice can be grown on the Plain and there is dairy farming. Spain, although mainly a dry, arid plateau, has coal and iron in the north and copper in the south.

This is a picture of a Europe teeming with people, its surface scarred heavily with large towns, industrial complexes, roads, railways and airfields, its bowels torn out by mining. It is a far cry from the Europe of the Stone Age, more or less covered with forests. The beginnings of this radical change from the one to the other are rooted in the change from man the hunter to man the tiller of the soil and the keeper of domestic stock. The hunter tends to conserve. If he does not he loses his livelihood. The pastoralist must destroy if he is to retain his livelihood. But at times the two combine to destroy, deliberately or inadvertently.

Seal sands, at the mouth of the Tees in northern England, showing a large industrial complex in the background. The birds (waders) in the estuary in the foreground are one of the few remaining features to remind us of how the region used to appear.

The beast of burden and general supplier of man's needs in the inhospitable north of Europe, the reindeer. Almost all Europe's reindeer are now domesticated. In the wild they live in herds of 20 to 30, migrating seasonally over distances of around 200 miles.

Tundra and taiga: twilight lands

The inhospitable tundra

In the extreme north is the tundra, represented in Europe by little more than a coastal strip extending northwards from about the level of Trondheim, in Norway, to the Kola Peninsula and the coasts of the White Sea and Barents Sea. The term tundra, from the Finnish word *tunturi*, is applied typically to flat, treeless country with a harsh climate, sparse vegetation and, in places, permanent frost not far below the surface, a wasteland with either bare hillocks of earth or, in low-lying areas, marshy soil. Along the tops of the mountain range forming the backbone of the Scandinavian Peninsula, however, similar conditions obtain and this is also included in the tundra. It corresponds also with the alpine zone of the mountains farther south. The sky over the tundra is often overcast; the winters are long and characterized by high winds that over large areas blow away the protective covering of snow. The few trees, such as dwarf birch and willow, are stunted and twisted by the winds. For the rest, the vegetation consists mainly of lichens.

Surprisingly, a few mammals continue to live in this inhospitable habitat without hibernating: the wolf, arctic fox, arctic hare, wolverine and ermine. Rodents are represented by the northern red-backed and grey-sided voles, and the arctic and Norway lemmings, which survive the winter by burrowing into snow. The arctic lemming is found as far north as Novaya Zemlya.

The voles eat any seeds, fruits or buds they can find, even bark and roots in winter, and any insect food available. The lemmings have an even wider diet and include in it moss, lichen and fungi, as well as carrion. Both form the main food of the carnivores and just as the populations of voles and lemmings are subject to cyclical rises and falls, reaching a peak every three years, on average, so the numbers of the predators rise and fall with them.

The most celebrated animal of northern Europe is the Norway lemming. This has been surrounded by legend and mystique ever since the sixteenth century when somebody explained that the sudden appearance of swarms of lemmings was due to their having dropped out of the skies. Later accounts, more sober but hardly less dramatic, told of columns of lemmings pouring down the mountainsides and committing mass suicide in the sea. This ancient legend persisted unchanged until recent times. Considerable attention has, however, been given by zoologists to this problem during the last decade, and although not all riddles have been solved the main cause for the rapid increases in numbers is now known to be climatic, linked with the lemmings' unusual winter breeding.

During the winter the lemmings shelter under the snow where they are protected from the cold, have adequate food and are more or less free of enemies apart from a few stoats and weasels. Each female is able to rear several litters. Provided the winter is not too prolonged there can be a high rate of survival but, as weather conditions are usually not propitious in spring, the normal occurrence is for many of the young to die of cold and for the total population numbers to remain stable.

Every few years conditions are right for a high survival rate of the young. There is a population explosion and large numbers of lemmings move down the mountainside in search of food. Their movements are random except where they meet a fork of a river, or some such obstacle, and the rodents are funnelled, so appearing to be moving in columns. They are preyed upon by foxes, stoats, weasels, ravens, rough-legged buzzards, the snowy owl and the longtailed skua. The real cause of the catastrophic drop in numbers, which brings the population back to normal, lies elsewhere. Probably as in other instances more systematically investi-

The typical home of the snowy owl is the arctic tundra and barren hills, but the bird irrupts southwards in large numbers every four years or so. It is then seen in a variety of habitats, on dunes and marshes, in open country or on sea and lake shores.

Norway lemmings survive in cold weather by burrowing under the snow, even breeding in winter. They eat a wide variety of food, including mosses, lichens, fungi and carrion.

The raven, large member of the crow family, feeding on a dead rabbit. Although absent from a large area of northern central Europe and much of Italy, the raven may elsewhere be found from the tundra to the Mediterranean shores.

gated, overcrowding of the habitat promotes fighting, failure to breed, disease and hunger.

In their movement down from the mountains the rodents seem to develop a psychosis akin to panic. Once this sets in they seem to go blindly ahead. Some of the lemmings do reach the sea and are drowned, as is usually described, especially in the fiords. Since the foot of the mountains in Norway is never far from the sea this is not surprising. It is this that gave rise to the stories of mass suicide in the sea. Lemmings will swim to cross a lake or river but if the water is at all choppy they drown. Any that enter the sea are almost certainly doomed since the surface is seldom flat calm.

Comparable in size to the rodents, although not in anything like the numbers, are the shrews, the common and pygmy shrews and the northern water shrew. These are insectivores, and invertebrates of most kinds are scarce, although spiders and mites are well represented and may reach very high densities. Other characteristic invertebrates of the tundra are the swarms of blood-sucking insects, few in species but astronomical in numbers so that people have to cover their heads with hoods and veils and take other measures to protect themselves.

By contrast, other insects are few. Inevitably, fleas are carried by the mammals. Bumblebees, with their furry bodies, are conspicuous. There are a few ants and beetles and only occasional dragon-flies; and at least several butterflies reach the tundra from farther south, the moorland clouded yellow, the small pearl-bordered fritillary and the Arran brown, to join the arctic and polar fritillaries.

The enormous numbers of lemmings, together with the other small mammals, are an index to the nutritious quality of the seemingly sparse vegetation. Another vegetarian mammal that cannot be called a rarity is the arctic hare, belonging to a species typical of mountain and alpine conditions elsewhere in Europe.

The arctic hare remains white throughout the year when living on the tundra, although in the taiga and on mountains farther south, where it is known as the varying, mountain or blue hare, it undergoes a change of coat from summer to winter. It is more gregarious than the brown hare and is well adapted to the extreme cold of winter by its thick fur, the hairy soles of its feet and its short ears and limbs. This hare feeds in winter on ground blown free of snow and is able when necessary to dig through deep snow to find the twigs of dwarf willow, the dry grasses and mosses which it eats.

The young of the arctic hare form an important part of the food of the arctic fox, an animal which has an extraordinary resistance to cold and which is found in the most inhospitable places. Nansen found one in the depths of winter on the ice-pack some 150 miles north of Novaya Zemlya. Others were observed during the winter of 1950–51 over 300 miles from the edge of the inland ice at the research station of the French Polar Expedition, in the centre of Greenland, at a height of over 3,000 metres, where temperatures reach –50°C.

The arctic fox spends all its life on solid ground, venturing on to the pack ice only infrequently. On the other hand, the polar bear is found on land only occasionally, for this animal passes practically the whole of its life on the ice. It is solitary except at the pairing season, and lives on the drifting pack, which has sometimes accidentally brought it even to Iceland and Norway. In January, the middle of the long arctic night, the female gives birth to two or three young in a crevasse, or a hole that she has dug in the snow. The young are no more developed at birth than those of the brown bear. They grow rapidly, nestled in the mother's thick fur, the whole family remaining in the winter den until March. In spring and summer the mother and young wander over the ice, stalking seals and young walruses or lying in wait for them at their breathing-holes.

The reindeer is perhaps the most characteristic species of the European tundra but as it is more numerous in the taiga it should be dealt with under that heading.

The only bird to remain on the tundra regularly throughout the year is the ptarmigan, a member of

Polar bears are now rare in Europe, though formerly they must have been much more numerous along the continent's northern shore. A thick layer of fat under the skin helps to keep them buoyant in the water and also keeps them warm.

Left: The arctic fox is almost symbolic of the polar fringes of the northern hemisphere, where the vegetation consists of lichens and mosses and dwarf, stunted trees. It feeds largely on the few small rodents hardy enough to inhabit the tundra and ekes out a living by scavenging.

The tundra of the subarctic has much in common with the tops of mountains, climatically and vegetationally. A typical animal resident of both is the ptarmigan, whose plumage changes to match its seasonally changing background: grey in summer, white in winter and grey with white in autumn.

The well-camouflaged arctic hare, like other small mammals living in the frozen north, has smaller extremities, notably the ears, than relatives living farther south. The smaller extremities mean less surface for the loss of body heat.

33

the grouse family, distinguished from other grouse by its white wings and white underparts. The plumage varies considerably at different seasons of the year and in winter both male and female are white all over except for the black tail and the cock's black eye patches. There is a red wattle over the eye which is larger in the male. In summer ptarmigan move about in family parties or flocks, feeding on shoots, leaves, seeds, berries and some insects. In winter they burrow under the snow to escape the worst of the cold.

The white winter plumage of the ptarmigan does more than serve as camouflage; it lowers the heat loss from the body. Ptarmigan have survived 40 degrees of frost.

The paucity of birds in winter contrasts strongly with the influx of summer migrants in June and July. Most of these breed on the marshes and lakes although some nest among the dwarf trees and lichens, like the little stint, which winters in equatorial or southern Africa under conditions that could hardly be more different from those under which it breeds. Many waders breed near the coast or on the shores of the lakes, the ringed plover being one of them. Dunlin, Jack snipe, the common sandpiper and Temminck's stint breed in

SAGE/ARDEA

The eider, a strongly maritime duck, breeds around the coasts of northern Europe. It is semi-domesticated for its down, especially in Iceland, and may be met as far south as Scotland and the Netherlands, with a colony on the west coast of France.

An inhabitant of sea coasts in winter, the black-throated diver nests commonly on the edges of large, deep inland lakes. It is widespread over Europe but breeds mainly in the north, especially in Scandinavia and northern Russia.

ROBERTS/ARDEA

The dunlin is Europe's commonest shore-bird. It is found as a migrant almost all over Europe but breeds mainly in the north, in Norway, much of the British Isles and along the Baltic coast, on high moors, bogs and salt marshes.

Both the golden eagle and the hooded crow are distributed widely over Europe, from extreme north to extreme south, although largely in different areas and habitats. The hooded crow is a habitual scavenger; golden eagles usually kill their prey, but they also eat carrion when it is available.

the bogs, the red-necked phalarope frequents the pools, and the ruffs hold their leks on the frozen peat mounds. During the brief spring the ground is carpeted with flowers the colours of which are rivalled by those of the bluethroats, lapland bunting, red-throated pipits and reed buntings. To these are added the arctic redpolls, snow buntings and the shore lark, with sand martins flying overhead.

Among larger birds, the lesser white-fronted and the bean goose graze the vegetation, and Bewick's swan swims on the pools, with the longtailed duck, blackthroated diver and king eider. On the coast the longtailed skua and pomarine skua harass the nesting birds, and the common gull brings up its young. Dominating all are the main predators, the snowy owl, the rough-legged buzzard and the gyrfalcon.

At the end of the short summer all depart southwards leaving only the ptarmigan and, occasionally, the snowy owl.

The northern pine forests

From the Scandinavian forests in the west, across Siberia to the Pacific Ocean in the east, stretches the largest forest in the world. It is made up mainly of conifers and has been named the taiga, from the Siberian word for it. Only a small part of it lies in Europe, but even that part is the largest area of forest in the continent, nearly 1,500 miles across, from Scandinavia to the Urals, and 800 miles or more from north to south. It is bounded in the north by tundra. In the south it meets the deciduous forest and there the two types of trees intermingle to form a mixed forest. The ground itself varies from spruce forest to moorlands and heaths carpeted with lichens or extensive beds of bilberry, broken with numerous lakes, peaty tarns and marshes, the whole interspersed with rivers and straggling groves of birches.

There are few species of trees, especially in the western half where only spruce and Scots pine grow. To the east of this, first larch, then Siberian fir and Siberian stone pine appear at longitudes 39°, 42° and 53° east respectively. The sequence is taken as an illustration of how the trees spread successively from Asia to Europe during the last postglacial period.

The taiga is a forest plain, for between the Scandinavian mountains to the west and the Urals to the east, nowhere is there high ground sufficient to break the visible contour of the conifers. The ash-grey surface soils of the taiga, with white sand beneath and brown loam below that, collectively known as podsol, are cold, acid from the thick carpet of needles accumulating on the ground, badly aerated and usually badly drained. The dense canopy above shuts out the light, and little other vegetation grows below. The soil is unfit for the production of crops except by the heavy use of fertilizers. In the mixed forest to the south, temperatures are high enough to promote the decomposition of lime-rich deciduous leaves to humus, yielding a dark soil favourable for agriculture.

Although some mammals belonging to the deciduous forests to the south are also found in the taiga, a few are rarely found elsewhere. The largest is the elk, the European counterpart of the North American moose, the largest of the deer family. A bull moose may be 2·1 m. at the shoulder with antlers spanning 1·8 m. It is awkward-looking with its long head, broad upper lip and tassel of hair and skin hanging from its throat. The female lacks antlers. At the rut, each male mates with several females. The elk's diet includes shoots, leaves, twigs and aquatic plants; in winter it eats largely bark. In summer elk spend many hours submerged in water or in mud wallows, probably as protection against the swarms of blood-sucking insects.

Smaller but more characteristic of the taiga, although it is also found in the tundra, is the reindeer, the deer that for so long has supplied most of the needs of people living in that harsh area. A mature bull stands 1·1 m. at the shoulder, the cows being 10–15 cm. less. It is the deer most utilized by man and in parts of its range has been domesticated. There are, for example, no wild reindeer left in Sweden. Reindeer live in herds of twenty to thirty and seasonally make migrations over distances of 200 miles. Domestication probably took place in the southern part of the animal's Asiatic range, before any other hoofed animal was domesticated, and this made possible man's settlement in the northern parts of Europe.

In winter reindeer feed mainly on lichens *(Cladonia* and *Cetraria)*, scraping the snow away with their hoofs to reach them. In the taiga they also eat lichens *(Usnea)* growing on trees, as well as buds and shoots of trees. In summer they eat sedges, grasses and broad-leaved herbaceous plants and occasionally birds' eggs and lemmings. Their main enemy is the wolf but young reindeer are also taken by lynx, wolverine, eagles and ravens.

Another large ungulate that penetrates into the

NORSTROM/N

A lapland forest of spruce, juniper and sallow. The spruce is *Picea abies*, the traditional North European Christmas tree. It is native to Scandinavia, the Alps and other mountain ranges throughout Europe.

The grey wolf is still found in isolated areas of Europe, particularly in the taiga. It feeds mainly on small mammals, but will also kill larger ones up to the size of an elk, and may attack domestic animals when food is scarce.

FERA/ZEFA

taiga, although it lives mainly in the deciduous forests farther south, is the red deer. In the forests its diet consists largely of leaves and shoots, and it undertakes considerable seasonal movements in some regions.

The brown bear nowadays finds one of its last refuges in the great boreal coniferous forests. It is a solitary animal, the males and females living apart except during the rutting season. Its diet is extremely varied: grass, leaves, buds, roots, wild bulbs; and often small rodents, insects, etc.

The brown bear lives in the conifer forests in winter, and is only found on the tundra in the warm season. During January the female gives birth to her two to three cubs in her winter den, and they stay with their mother for a long time, often for two years. Each adult lives in a territory of some seven to eight square miles and defends it vigorously against others of the same sex.

The grey wolf (or timber wolf in North America) has a wider range than probably any other mammal, and although it ranges through the temperate coniferous forests, it also ranges over the plains and tundra of Asia and North America and is scattered over Europe. Therefore, although this chapter is concerned with the taiga, it is not practicable, in

Right: The European brown bear had supplanted the Cave bear by the later years of the Old Stone Age (Paleolithic). Now rare itself, it lives in conifer forests in winter, moving to the tundra in summer. Its varied diet includes grass, leaves, roots and small rodents and insects.

A bull elk, close relative of the better known North American moose, in its typical habitat of marsh, moor and coniferous forest. In summer elks eat shoots, leaves, twigs and aquatic plants; in winter bark is their main food.

GRAHN/N

writing of the wolf, to ignore its distribution elsewhere in Europe.

Everywhere its numbers have been drastically reduced, most of all in Europe, where wolves were probably very numerous when man first started to colonize the continent. Today the wolf survives precariously in Scandinavia and northern Finland and in eastern and southern European Russia, in the Balkans, Italy and Sicily, and the Iberian peninsula. The last killed in France were in the Massif Central in 1939, in the Côte d'Or in 1946, and in Isère in 1954. In Switzerland a male wolf was killed in Valais in 1947.

This tally of its European toeholds is deceptive. In Sweden where it is hunted with helicopters and snow scooters there are fewer than 40 remaining. In the U.S.S.R. a vigorous anti-wolf campaign is sustained outside the national parks, so although the exact numbers are not known they cannot be high. In the Spanish sierras it is rare everywhere. It maintains a hold in the mountains of Sicily and although in theory it is confined to the Parco Nazionale d'Abruzzo in the Apennines, in fact it is found over a fairly wide range, the family parties being mobile and ranging widely. There are pockets of wolves in northern and southern Yugoslavia, in northern Albania, Macedonia and adjacent areas of Bulgaria. In the southern Carpathians and the Caucasus wolves are more strongly represented and they are found throughout the waterlogged lands of the Danube delta, especially in the woodlands of the island of Letea.

The present-day picture of the wolf in Europe is a striking illustration of what can happen to a species

GOODERS/ARDEA

under intense persecution. Its members take refuge in inaccessible places, such as mountains, forests and islands. They may leave the mountains for the lowlands under pressure of severe winter, but in the Danube delta the wolf has shown more especially the adaptability of the species that has ensured its survival throughout its range, even if in limited numbers. In the delta it has become semi-aquatic, at home in the reed-beds, even able to climb trees. So marked is its change in habits it is regarded by the Rumanians as a distinct species, the reed wolf.

The last wolf was killed in England between the years 1485 and 1509. The last in Scotland was killed in 1743, and in Ireland in the 1960s. A wolf trailed in Alaska was seen to travel 700 miles in six weeks, exemplifying the wandering nature of this beast, and explaining its sporadic appearance unexpectedly in wolf-free localities in Europe. So a wolf can conceivably turn up almost anywhere on continental Europe today, although it is an extremely rare occurrence.

The lynx *(Felis lynx)*, another mammal typical of the taiga, is also rare today. Formerly it probably ranged over the whole of Europe. Today it is found in Scandinavia, Finland, northern Russia, the Balkans and Spain, mostly in the mountains.

Lynxes in southern Europe are heavily spotted, especially those in Spain, which have long been considered as belonging to a separate species *(F. pardina)*. This view is no longer held.

A medium-sized member of the cat family, with tufted ears, the lynx is solitary and nocturnal, hunting rabbits, hares, rodents, foxes, badgers, ground birds, fish and insects. Young deer are also taken, as well as domestic dogs and cats. In fact, its wide range of prey has set man's hand against it once he started keeping domestic stock. And the lynx has an Achilles' heel under pressure of persecution. The kittens stay with and are dependent on the mother for a year. They retain their milk teeth, and their claws meanwhile do not develop, for nine months. If the mother is killed, the young are doomed. They cannot kill even small rodents.

Even without an Achilles' heel, continued human persecution can be disastrous, as with the wolverine, which survives today mainly in the mountains of Sweden and in smaller numbers in the forests of the taiga. The glutton, as it is alternatively called, is the largest of the weasel family, almost like a small bear. It feeds especially on carrion, but will kill almost anything it meets. Its fighting qualities, coupled with a marked propensity for robbing the

The lynx, the bob-tailed member of the cat family, is most at home in the coniferous forests. Distinguished by its tufted ears, it is credited with unusually keen sight.

Europe's one flying squirrel is an inhabitant of the taiga with a curiously limited range. It is found in Finland but not in Scandinavia. It is also found south to the Baltic provinces but only as far west as the Polish boundary.

NORSTRÖM/N

The wolverine, largest of the weasel family, has incurred wrath by its habit of robbing hunters' traps, and also because it will kill almost any animal large, medium or small. Its supposedly insatiable appetite is reflected in its alternative name, the glutton.

Pine marten stealing eggs. These do not form its staple diet, although eggs are always at risk in its presence. Its normal prey is squirrels which it pursues through the trees with slightly greater agility than its quarry possesses.

MCGASKILL/AFA

traps of fur-trappers, have made it singularly unpopular. Its aggressiveness is such that it will fight, and usually defeat, lynx, bear and wolf.

The weasel family (Mustelidae) is particularly well represented in the taiga, with the otter, pine marten, stoat and weasel throughout, the badger in the southern half and the sable and European mink in the east. The marten, being a skilled climber, preys largely on the red squirrel, which is widespread in the coniferous forests as it is elsewhere throughout continental Europe. It also takes small rodents, eggs, birds, frogs, insects and occasionally buds and wild fruits. The other smaller mustelids live mainly on ground-dwelling rodents, the voles and lemmings, to which may occasionally be added the three shrews, the pygmy, common and masked shrews and, in the southern reaches of the taiga, the common mole. Rats and mice are not a feature of the taiga except in its southern parts, although the ubiquitous and alien brown rat is found throughout. Voles and lemmings are numerous, the lemming and wood lemming being distributed from Scandinavia to the Kola Peninsula. The bank vole and the field vole reach as far as the northern limit of the taiga in Russia. The flying squirrel lives in the northern forests from Finland to Siberia. It is nocturnal, its diet a mixture of seeds, toadstools, eggs, fledgelings and insects, and it shelters during the day in old nests or in holes in trees.

Bats are few in the taiga. The northern bat (*Eptesicus nilssonii*) is found more or less throughout, and the whiskered bat and a very few others are intermittently distributed.

Since the taiga is heavily forested there is an

DALTON/NHPA

SMITH/ARDEA

Unmistakable from its pinkish-chestnut crest, yellow-tipped tail and the 'sealing-wax' red tips to its secondary wing feathers, the waxwing is a typical taiga species. It breeds in northern Scandinavia, Finland and Russia, in pine forests and birch woods.

Right: Redstarts, beautiful members of the thrush family, are widely spread throughout Europe, except in the extreme west. They feed their nestlings mainly on caterpillars.

Left: Highly destructive of grassland when its numbers reach a peak, the field vole is numerous from the arctic coast to the Pyrenees and Alps and eastwards to the Yenesei river. Its high rate of reproduction makes it the prey of numerous carnivores.

Bank voles are found all over northern and central Europe, reaching the Mediterranean in southern France. Berries and seeds collected on the woodland floor or in the hedgerow are an important part of their diet.

BURTON/COLEMAN

BEVAN/ARDEA

abundance of small song birds, many of which are common throughout Europe. There are many tits, including the crested, Siberian and willow tits, the latter being the most common. Siskins and red-polls are to be expected; and the chaffinch, brambling and bullfinch are there also. Warblers are well represented, notably willow warbler, chiff-chaff, and arctic warbler. Redstart, red-wing and song thrush are present in the southern parts. More typical of the pine forests are the wax-wing, pine grosbeak, and three species of crossbill, the common, parrot and two-barred, with their crossed bills adapted for extracting seeds from pine cones.

That most showy of ground birds, the caper-caillie has its headquarters in the taiga forests while the black grouse is met on the boggy ground around the forests. In the forests, also, are four woodpeckers, the lesser and great spotted, the three-toed and the black woodpecker, black with a red crest, that feeds mainly on ants, and especially the wood ant that makes nest mounds of pine needles. The most characteristic is, however, the three-toed woodpecker which is found in Scan-dinavia as well as the taiga of Finland and northern Russia. It is also found in the mountainous forests

SMITH/ARDEA

A male crossbill feeding its young. With its bill adapted to taking seeds out of pine cones, the crossbill is inevitably tied to coniferous forests. Although a typical taiga species, it may be found else-where in Europe.

Black grouse displaying. Their displays at the 'lek', an open space in a forest or a grassy patch on moorland, are well known. The cocks threaten each other, fanning their tails and fluffing the white feathers underneath, lowering their heads and exposing their red wattles—all part of the breeding ritual.

GRAHN/N

MURRAY/NHPA

MCGREGOR/COLEMAN

ROBERTS/ARDEA

ROBERTS/ARDEA

A sedge warbler bringing a fly to its nestlings among the reeds. Its untidy nest is built among dense vegetation near water and in swampy thickets. Widespread over most of Europe, it breeds in suitable places right up to the arctic coast.

Top: The great spotted woodpecker is more at home in broad-leaved trees but may also frequent pinewoods. Widespread throughout Europe from the taiga southwards, the mating call is a rapid drumming made by both sexes on the branches of trees.

The American name of marsh hawk more fittingly describes the hen harrier, a bird of prey, ranging through northern and central Europe and south-westwards to the Iberian peninsula. It nests on the ground on moors and in swamps and thickets.

Top: The tawny-grey Siberian jay is one of the characteristic arboreal birds of the taiga of Europe, in the coniferous and birch woods. Its food is the seeds of pines and Siberian cedars, berries, insects, mice and the eggs and young of small birds.

of Central Europe and the Balkans, suggesting that this species moved northwards in the post-glacial period, following up the retreat of the ice-cap, and left behind relict faunas in the mountain (or alpine) taiga. This woodpecker needs an abundance of old rotting pines.

Those preying on these small birds include the great grey shrike and the Siberian jay, the latter a nest-robber rather than a true predator, but one which adds colour to the woodland scene. The true predators are the goshawk and the owls, especially the great grey owl, the eagle owl, Tengmalm's owl and the hawk owl.

The bogs and marshes of the taiga are many, and so are the lakes, where the sedge warbler and the reed bunting nest, near waders such as the greenshank and spotted redshank and numerous ducks. The latter include mallard, widgeon, pintail, shoveler, tufted duck, the smew, goosander and red-breasted merganser. The whooper swan is another taiga waterfowl.

Birds of prey include the hen harrier, and the osprey is found wherever there are lakes. The osprey, feeding exclusively on fish, has the choice of perch, pope, whitefish *(Coregonus)*, grayling, brown trout, burbot and pike.

The characteristic insects of pine forests are beetles, that bore into the wood or under the bark. Two types alone suffice to exemplify these, the longicorn beetles and the ambrosia beetles, both of which have special peculiarities.

The longicorn beetles constitute a large and important family the members of which, for the most part, spend their larval life tunnelling in and

feeding upon timber. They have unusually long antennae. Some have a superficial resemblance to wasps and the adults of these fly by day. The others are nocturnal. A typical example is the timberman, *Acanthocinus aedilis*, distributed widely over Europe, and especially in the northern half. It often turns up in cargoes of timber, far from its normal habitat.

The timberman is 18 mm. long, grey dappled with brown, and the male's antennae are 75 mm. long. The antennae of the female are less than half this length. When she is about to lay she bites a deep pit in the bark of a pine, inserts her ovipositor and lays her eggs in it. The larva tunnels under the bark for two to three years then pupates, the pupal stage lasting three to four weeks, beginning at the end of summer. The imago, or adult insect, is then ready to emerge, but does not do so until the following spring. Until the beetle leaves the pupal case the long antennae are folded in a complicated series of loops and turns.

These long antennae are characteristic of beetles living in forests but their function is uncertain. An early theory is that they are used as callipers, by which the insect measures the girth of a tree, to determine whether it is of suitable size in which to lay eggs. One argument against this is that the female, responsible for the laying, has much shorter antennae.

Timber beetles of another family (Scolytidae) are called bark beetles, or more commonly ambrosia beetles. They are very small and live in tunnels in live trees feeding, not on the wood, but on a fungus or "ambrosia" living on the sap, the spores of the fungus having been carried in by the beetles on their bodies when they tunneled their way in to lay. The adults feed the fungus to their larvae and they tend them in other ways, as for example, by removing their faeces from the tunnels. Some species of ambrosia beetles carefully prepare a substratum of larval faeces or wood chips on which they nurture the fungus, even weeding out other species of fungus not required. It is not surprising to find, in such "advanced" insects, that some species show an exaggerated polygamy: one male to sixty females.

Right: A longhorn beetle *Prionus coriarius* on bark. Of the 13,000 species of longhorn, or longicorn, beetles few are found in Europe, where they tend to be known as 'the timberman'. They lay their eggs in the trunks of trees and in these the larvae bore.

A golden eagle's eyrie with one well-grown eaglet. Carcasses of small prey, including lemmings, litter the nest. Golden eagles take a variety of small mammals, and some larger birds such as grouse and ptarmigan. Young sheep and deer, even carrion, may form part of their diet.

The osprey breeds mainly in northern Europe but ranges south outside the breeding season. It spends much of its time perched on a tree taking wing from time to time over water. On sighting a fish it pauses in mid-air to dive, entering the water feet-first, with half-closed wings, to secure its prey with its talons.

BURTON/COLEMAN

PAYSAN

The primeval green larder

The ancient primeval forest was an uneven-aged, self-regenerating forest, a high canopy forest in which the standard trees formed a more or less continuous upper stratum with occasional gaps letting in light. Below was a discontinuous stratum of subsidiary shrubs and young trees. This is not to say the forest itself would have been continuous. There would have been much marsh between, and there would have been pathways and clearings formed by the larger animals, the aurochs, wild horse, bison, red deer and brown bear.

Unfortunately for the naturalist, the area of deciduous forest corresponds very largely to the main areas of ancient civilization and later industrialization. As a result, even the fragments of forest that remain contain only an impoverished mammalian fauna. Most of the large hoofed animals are gone as well as the carnivores. The aurochs was the wild ox, half as big again as a Hereford bull, with long spreading horns. The bulls were black, with a white stripe along the back, a white or greyish muzzle and white curly hair between the horns. The cows were brownish-red with a brown or fawn saddle. Early Stone Age man hunted the aurochs; later Stone Age man domesticated it, to give a beast of burden and our present-day dairy cattle. The last aurochs died in a Polish park in 1627 but the species had disappeared in the wild over most of Europe long before that, although it was still abundant in the Vosges under the Merovingians (A.D. 500 to 750).

The European bison or wisent must also have been widespread. It survived in the Vosges until the seventh century and in Switzerland until the eleventh century. Less shaggy and slightly smaller than the better-known North American bison, a full-grown bull weighed a tonne. The wisent has

Previous page: The leaf litter on the deciduous forest floor is home to some of the more favoured items of the badger's diet, and badger sets are mainly located under trees. Their food includes insects, earthworms, snails and slugs, tubers, bulbs, nuts and other fallen fruits.

Right: Little is left of the original broad-leaved forests that once covered so much of central and western Europe. Burnham beeches, shown here, in southern England, may be a remnant of virgin forest.

Deciduous forest contrasts with pine forests more especially in its ground cover. A carpet of pine needles tends to inhibit undergrowth. A layer of leaf litter encourages shrubs, grass and herbaceous flowers, except under beech trees, where the ground is bare.

ORR

The European wild ox, the aurochs, has long been extinct. The ancestor of today's dairy cattle, it was hunted for meat before being domesticated as a beast of burden.

HERBERT/NSP

51

been wiped out except for a few preserved in the Bielowecza forest in Poland, but it and the aurochs both figure in the cave-paintings of south-west Europe. These two alone would have trodden broad paths through the forest.

Trees have an importance to any region's ecology, which is normally only realized in a vague way, usually in the form that trees give out oxygen by day, so purifying the air. Their value goes much further. In broad-leaved forests the yearly accumulation of dead leaves results in a rich black loam. The canopy in a mixed forest is less dense than in a pinewood. Light is let in, which promotes growth of shrubs and bushes. This undergrowth gives shelter to large numbers of birds and small mammals. Trees prevent soil erosion by binding the soil with their roots and by preventing the run-off of rainwater. The leaves, twigs and branches check the fall of raindrops and the "drip" that continues after the rain has ceased ensures the maximum absorption of water by the ground beneath. Where broken and rotting branches lie on the ground, these act as a sponge to absorb moisture and slowly release it to the soil.

The roots of deciduous trees penetrate deeply. They help aerate the soil, a process that is assisted

Pennywort, with its umbrella-like leaves and tall racemes of greenish-yellow flowers has long figured in medicinal herbals for treatment of scalds and burns. Its juice was also said to have soothing properties. Overshadowing the pennywort is the end of a fallen tree trunk, its annual rings etched by a fungus.

by earthworms, moles and other burrowing animals. They bring up from deep in the soil minerals in solution which later are returned to the top soil in the fallen leaves. Water is brought up also and given off into the air by the leaves, 20 kg. of beech leaves, for example, giving out 95·2 kg. or 95 litres of water each day in summer. Trees provide shelter for plants and animals, against rain, wind and frost, as well as food for many animals. Above all, the surviving remnants of Europe's virgin deciduous forests show that the ancient forests represented a maximum productive capacity of the soil, surpassed only by the tropical rain forests.

Two examples will suffice to illustrate the food supply that trees represent. The first is the oak and its acorns. According to the Roman naturalist Pliny, acorns were then the chief wealth of many

52

The hazel dormouse is most commonly found in hazel bushes, where it collects the nuts, but acorns and berries also form part of its diet.

Bullfinches are often disliked for their destruction of fruit buds in early spring. They feed their nestlings on insects only, regurgitating these in a half-digested mass into the youngsters' throats.

nations. This sounds like an exaggeration to modern ears. Yet the oak was originally valued in other parts of Europe and in later ages for the acorns it produced, for feeding cattle and pigs. In the time of the Greek geographer Strabo, pigs from Gaul, fattened on acorns, were traded in Rome. The famous Laws of the Twelve Tables, engraved on copper and posted on the Senate House in Rome, in 450 B.C., proclaimed that a man was entitled to collect any acorns fallen from his own trees onto a neighbour's land. In Saxon England, and for centuries after this, swine and cattle were fed on acorns, and even human beings ate them in times of scarcity.

The second example concerns ash seeds. A number of birds as well as small mammals rely on these for their winter food. Ash seeds are important

It is understandable that plants should have brightly coloured fruits to attract animals to eat them, so spreading the seeds. It seems an act of providence, however, to endow fruits like the blackberry with a rich store of vitamins and energizing food.

Right: The earlier naturalists were surprised to discover that, in addition to nuts and berries, squirrels eat a variety of fungi. Biochemical research has, however, shown fungi to be highly nutritious. This picture, almost symbolic of the squirrel's habits, shows the rodent eating a nut, surrounded by the sulphur-capped toadstool.

The fungus *Polyporus* attacking a dead tree trunk fallen on the forest floor. Fungi are the main agent in returning the substance of trees to the earth, enriching the humus. New trees grow best where this has happened.

to the bullfinch, and when the crop fails, as it does every few years, the bird turns to buds. In woodlands the number of buds is high so only a small proportion is taken. In an orchard, or a garden, a failure of ash seeds means the bullfinches strip the trees of buds, and in extreme cases there is no blossom.

Since Europe was once largely covered with forests it follows that the indigenous animals must originally have been mainly forest-dwellers, although today they are commonly found elsewhere, because of the destruction of the forests. They must also have found other sustenance in the forests, in addition to obvious fruits such as acorns, nuts and berries. A surprising food source is the woodland fungi.

Fungi are more important than is normally realized in the life and death of forests. Some assist the nutrition of trees. These are the mycorrhiza, an association of fungal threads growing on the outside of the roots of trees, or growing into them, passing food materials to the tree. Others are serious in attacking living trees, and the rest are essential agents of decay and the formation of humus.

The damaging part of a fungus is that which

generally passes unseen, the slender threads known as the hyphae. The fruiting body, which is the toadstool, mushroom or bracket fungus, often provides food for animals, from flies to squirrels. Most wild animals eat some kind of fungi, even wolves and bears. So do domesticated cattle. Reindeer dig fungi from under the snow, and in parts of Finland it was long the practice to feed cattle on fresh or salted toadstools; elsewhere they have been used as fodder for pigs and poultry. Analysis of the common toadstool *Boletus edulis*, as well as the cultivated mushroom, has shown they are richer in protein than any dried vegetable except nuts. In an experiment, rats that were fed mainly on mushrooms for six weeks gained weight.

Although toadstools are mainly eighty-four to ninety-two per cent water they contain nitro-genous materials, carbohydrates, fat and minerals. The last of these are mainly potassium and phospheric acid with small quantities of sodium, calcium, magnesium, iron, manganese, aluminium, silica, sulphur and chlorine. The chemical analyses of fungi vary with the species and there is variation in the conclusions drawn from them. Some scientists claim fungi are as rich in proteins as meat. The analyses also show they are rich in vitamins. All fungi contain the vitamin B complex, while the antirachitic vitamin D, which is absent from green vegetables, is present in appreciable quantities. Vitamin A is present in fair amounts in some toadstools but absent from many others, and the ascorbic vitamin C is only occasionally present and then in small amounts.

Whether fungi contribute to the larger size of

the red deer in continental Europe, the fact remains that there is a marked difference in size between them and the red deer of Great Britain. Owing to the destruction of broad-leaved forests in Britain, the red deer live mainly on moors and graze rather than browse. Their body size is less and the antlers smaller. This was made evident some years ago by the discovery of a cache of antlers in Hampton Court Palace. The antlers were from deer killed in the sixteenth century. They were noticeably bigger than the largest in Britain today and more like the antlers of red deer that browse in forests in central Europe.

The brown bear is another animal of the primeval forests of Europe, and, like the red deer, it has suffered a curtailment of its range. It disappeared from England in the eleventh century, from Switzerland in 1904, and from the French Alps in 1937. About seventy still remained in some of the French Pyrenean valleys in 1953. It is seriously threatened in the Abruzzi, but is protected in Swedish Lapland, and is still relatively abundant in the Carpathians, in Slovakia, Croatia, Bosnia, Bulgaria, and particularly in some places in Russia.

Although the brown bears of the northern

Left: Red deer are typically forest animals although where forests have been destroyed they live on open moors. They inhabit mainly the deciduous forests of central Europe but extend northwards into southern Scandinavia, to the British Isles, and southwards to north-west Africa.

The crab spider *Misumera vatia* settles in a yellow flower, changing colour to match its background. Perfectly camouflaged, it waits for an unsuspecting insect to alight.

CALLOW/NHPA

hemisphere have been given many species names and several vernacular names, zoologists are now realizing they all belong to one species. They have been given many names because they differ in colour and size. The grizzly bear, for example, is larger than the European brown bear, and the Kodiak and Kenai bears of Alaska are huge beasts, weighing 700 kg. or more. The larger size of the Alaskan bears is probably the result of climate. There is a general tendency towards an increase in body size in the colder latitudes. The much smaller size of present-day brown bears in Europe is more likely due to overkill and partly also to impoverishment of the diet. That bears in Europe used to grow to a much larger size is evident from the sizes of skins preserved in museums in Russia.

Because man today does not live in forests but builds his houses where the ground has been largely cleared of trees, his perspective on the distribution of bird species tends to be warped. A walk across country shows that birds are concentrated in woods, around houses (except where these are themselves concentrated in towns) and wherever there is water, especially on and around lakes. The countryside between tends to be barren of birds. Those that take up residence around houses are particularly numerous as to species where there are clumps of trees, and the birds are those that live naturally in forest fringes and in clearings in the forest.

Woodpeckers are the birds most characteristic of woodlands proper. There are nine species in Europe, although only three have reached the British Isles. The richness of the woodland diet and the woodpeckers' ability to take a wide range of food in woodlands can be exemplified by cataloguing the diet of the great spotted woodpecker. It takes all kinds of insects and their larvae living in bark or in the wood beneath it, especially those of beetles and moths. In addition it takes the larvae of flies, gall insects and the wood wasp. Spiders are taken, and young birds and birds' eggs laid in cavities in trees. It also eats beechmast, acorns, hazels, pine seeds, apple pips, cherries and rowan berries, as well as almond stones, wedging these in crevices in bark and hammering them with the beak to split them open.

The history of the woodpeckers in Europe shows how the fortunes of an animal can be closely linked with changes in the vegetation. The Syrian woodpecker, near relative of the great spotted, one of the nine mentioned, belongs to south-west Asia and was first recorded in Europe in 1890, in

Female great spotted woodpecker. Woodpeckers take a wide range of food from their woodland habitat. The great spotted woodpecker takes insects and their larvae from the bark and wood of trees, spiders, young birds and eggs, and a variety of fruits and seeds.

The green woodpecker, known for its call which resembles maniacal laughter, is widely distributed over central and southern Europe. Unlike other woodpeckers it tends to feed on the ground, on ants taken from their underground galleries and insect grubs from rotten stumps.

Bulgaria. It bred in Hungary for the first time in 1939, reached the Slovakian Carpathians in 1949, south of Vienna in 1951 and west of Krems on the Danube in 1953. In south-east Europe, the great spotted woodpecker is only thinly present and the species appears to have come into Europe in response to an increase in the area of cultivated land. The great spotted woodpecker in that region is found mainly in mountain forests. Where, in mountain oak forests, it is absent, the Syrian woodpecker has penetrated.

In the post-glacial period the white-backed woodpecker seems to have spread across Europe from Asia. Then came the destruction of the forests leaving relict groups of this species in the Pyrenees and the Abruzzi mountains in Italy. The middle spotted woodpecker in the post-glacial period spread into Central Europe from the Iberian peninsula, where it had barely survived

the last Ice Age. Its range was almost identical with that of the hornbeam, a tree characteristic of the European forest. With deforestation and the planting of pine forests, the distribution of the middle spotted woodpecker has become patchy.

The green woodpecker is found practically all over Europe except in the north. It feeds on insects living in bark but also feeds on the ground, on insect larvae and especially ants. The last of the European woodpeckers, the grey-headed woodpecker, is very like the green, except for the grey head, and it also feeds on trees and, on the ground, on ants. It seems that the grey-headed came into Europe from Asia in post-glacial times and has since been spreading slowly across the continent. Competition between these two birds of such similar habits seems to be avoided by the two living among different types of trees and by the grey-headed being more of a forest-dweller.

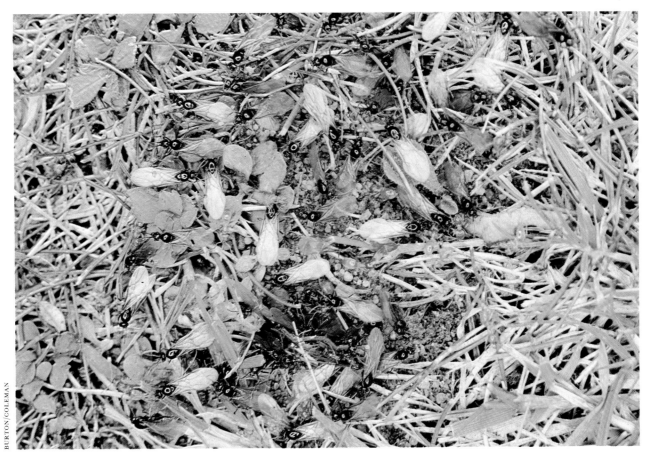

BURTON/COLEMAN

Males, or drones, of the meadow ant *Lasius flava* emerging for their nuptial flight. The queens and males mature some time in advance of the flight but are restrained by the workers until weather conditions are just right.

In places pure deciduous forests are replaced by mixed woodlands. There, as well as in pine forests, occur the conspicuous mounds of pine needles, the nests of the wood ant *Formica rufa*. These mounds may be almost 1 metre high and 2 metres across the base.

DALTON/NHPA

Climax vegetation and its smaller inhabitants

The large primeval forests of Europe, for the most part, grew where the ice-cap or the tundra then fringing them had rested. In the natural reclamation of the ground, as it dried out, a succession of vegetation appeared. The first were the lichens, which can grow everywhere except in the soot-laden atmosphere of large industrial towns, even in polar regions where no other plants can survive. They are the main element in the tundra vegetation. So-called reindeer moss *(Cladonia)*, supporting large reindeer and caribou herds, is a lichen.

Each lichen is made up of two plants, unicellular algae and fungus living in close association. The fungus takes in moisture and also gives out substances that dissolve the rock, the mineral then being absorbed. The algae manufacture sugars from carbon dioxide in the air in the pre-

HAWKES/NHPA

Song thrushes eat insects, worms and berries but their favourite diet is snails. A thrush holds the shell and hammers it on a hard surface, a flat stone, piece of metal or glass to smash it.

TWEEDIE/NHPA

The common garden snail, its shell frequently seen broken on a thrush's 'anvil', is *Helix aspersa*. Although it commonly damages garden plants its natural role is that of composter, eating dying or dead vegetation and returning waste from this to the general humus of the soil.

sence of sunlight. A dying lichen combined with rock particles continue the soil building, so that mosses and, later, ferns can thrive. These are followed by small herbaceous plants, shrubs and trees, in succession, over long periods of time, the trees representing the climax in this succession.

Other organisms contribute to the formation of soil. Bacteria help to break down the plant material, and other nitrogen-fixing bacteria add the fertilizing nitrates. As the plant succession progresses, mites, woodlice and soil insects play their part in breaking up the dead leaves and other products of dead plants. The soil insects are mostly microscopic in size and countless in numbers. It has been estimated that the total weight of soil insects, mites and woodlice in the world is equal to nine times the weight of the human population. To bring this down to more comprehensible terms, the number in a square metre of grassland is 341,000 and in natural heathland 570,000. In arable land it is least, at 26,000, and in spruce plantation, 155,000.

As the soil formation progresses it gathers momentum rapidly, as the plant cover increases and the animals living on it multiply. Animal droppings and carcasses are added to the plant humus, much of the material being broken down by a wealth of fungi, made obvious by the coloured caps of toadstools. Slugs and snails feed on the fungi and leaf litter, earthworms drag leaves into the ground, millipedes and some of the larger insects add to the breaking down process, all of these being more numerous in the soil of deciduous forests than elsewhere. Insects of many kinds find their niches in the forest, in the soil and vege-

Right: A male blackbird bringing insect food to its young. There is strong sexual dimorphism in this species. The mature male is glossy black with a bright yellow bill. The hen is brown with a speckled throat and a darker bill.

The song thrush sings for most of the year in a variety of habitats, including cultivated gardens. It usually feeds on the ground, hopping and running along, stopping from time to time to listen for worms in the soil.

ARDEA

tation, attracting birds and small mammals to the feast.

That this picture is not overdrawn is evidenced by the long list of perching birds living today in the broad-leaved forests, some in the heart of the woodland, others on the fringes where the trees thin out. Some use the woodlands for part of the year, others have become more adapted to parkland or feed in the clearings, using the undergrowth or the trees for nesting. On the ground various thrushes search the leaf litter: the blackbird, song thrush and redwing. The robin haunts the clearings, the nightingale the scrub. The hawfinch, shyest of birds, disappears into cover at the slightest disturbance after cracking open the hornbeam seeds that litter the ground, to swallow the kernels. The common wren has earned the name troglodyte, a cave-dweller, because it keeps to the darkest recesses. The ubiquitous chaffinch searches the ground for seeds. It can be found in woods, but equally it is at home in gardens or on arable land after the corn has been cut.

Warblers of many kinds, the wood warbler, blackcap, chiffchaff and lesser whitethroat among them, search the branches and the leaves for insects and feed on berries in season, while filling the air with their melodies. Tree creepers fly to the bases of the trees and run mouse-like up the trunks, searching and probing the crevices of the bark as they go for insects and spiders. Nuthatches work the bark downwards, sideways or upwards as the mood takes them, hacking at the bark or picking out insects or spiders from the crevices with their pick-like bills. Tits, with their tiny beaks, do much the same job of cleaning the tree trunks and the bushes of smaller insects.

Where small birds nest there will live the nest-robbing jay; but a jay has other tastes besides. It eats large numbers of acorns in autumn and when these are ripe the woods resound to the raucous cries of jays in the oaks. Jays also bury acorns and can go straight to a buried acorn even when the ground is covered with snow. They do not eat all they bury. Some get left, to germinate and help in the regeneration of the woodlands.

Only the small mammals seem to have suffered little from changes in the vegetation, some having benefited from them. Moles and hedgehogs are plentiful on cultivated ground and red-toothed and musk shrews are widely distributed in fields, as well as copses and woods.

Shrews, voles and mice are all mouse-sized.

Male hawfinch on an alder branch. Hawfinches are the shyest of birds, less seen than the results of their feeding, such as cherry stones and other hard seeds lying on the ground neatly split into two by the powerful bill.

Left: The robin is inclined to keep close to human habitation and to anyone digging, both habits leading to friendliness between bird and man. The habits spring from an inborn tendency to be attracted to large animals that disturb the ground with their hoofs, exposing insects and worms.

The common wren at its nest, feeding three young. This small bird with its upstanding tail pours out a volume of song disproportionate to its size. It feeds typically on spiders and insects caught around the bases of shrubs and bushes.

Shrews can be recognized by their tapering snouts, small eyes and small ears. They are remarkable for their short life-span, fifteen months maximum. Also, the pygmy white-toothed shrew, of the Mediterranean region is the smallest mammal, 3·7 cm. long with the tail 2·5 cm. Another white-toothed shrew, the common, has become famous of recent years for its caravanning. When a litter of young are nearing the weaning stage they go out with the mother following in line. The first baby holds the mother, near the base of her tail with its teeth. Each baby then holds the one in front in the

same way. So the whole family proceeds, in step, holding so firmly that the mother can be lifted with her family hanging from her.

Voles, more mouse-like still, have blunt, rounded muzzles, small eyes and ears. They eat plant food, unlike shrews that eat mainly insects, as well as a few seeds. The bank vole eats grass, roots, bulbs, fruits and seeds, occasionally an insect or a snail, or even carrion. The field vole, which also lives in woods, eats grass, sedges and the like, while the common vole, more commonly found today in grasslands, feeds on grass.

These voles, and the shrews, are varied in their habitat and are prepared to live where their food is, whether it is in woods, fields or gardens. The wood mouse, also called the longtailed field mouse, is the same. It eats any kind of berry, nut or seed,

Cock chaffinch feeding its hungry young. Chaffinches occur throughout Europe except in the extreme north. Although originally birds of woodlands and forest edges they have adapted well to farmlands and gardens. Outside the breeding season they live in flocks, often males in one flock and females in another.

BLEWITT/ARDEA

The great tit is common throughout Europe except for the extreme north, especially in deciduous woods where it feeds on insects, fruits and buds. It has readily adapted to parks and gardens and has become a first favourite at bird feeding tables.

The tree creeper, with its long down-curved bill searches the crevices of bark for insects and spiders. Its typical behaviour is to ascend the tree in a spiral, clinging by its strong toes and supported by its tail.

BLACKBURN/NHPA

often hoarding them in large quantities in the ground, like its near relative, the more robust yellow-necked mouse, with a yellow or orange patch on its chest. The second of these lives throughout the zone of broad-leaved trees but extends north into Sweden and Finland and south-east into the Russian steppes. In the Mediterranean region it lives in the hills but is absent from Iberia and Italy. In France and the Low Countries it is confined to the eastern strip and in the British Isles lives only in southern England and Wales. Yet it is so like the wood mouse, which is so widely distributed, as often to be mistaken for it.

Another widespread insectivore of the broad-leaved forests is the common mole. This exploits the surface layers down to over a metre, feeding mainly on earthworms but also taking subterranean insect larvae. Its burrowing serves to aerate the soil and turn it over, the equivalent of man's ploughing but at a slower tempo.

The vegetation of the broad-leaved forests provides a rich soil and in or on this supports a wealth of small phytophages (herbivores), from minute insects to the voles. Larger phytophages are the hare, now associated more with open grassland but originally feeding in open woodland, the rabbit and the omnivorous but mainly herbivorous wild boar that supplements the ploughing activities of the mole by turning over the earth with its snout.

Above the ground, in the coarse herbage, lives the harvest mouse, feeding on seeds, and higher still the shrubs of the undergrowth are exploited by dormice, feeding on nuts and berries mainly, occasionally taking insects. The hazel dormouse uses the bark of honeysuckle for its nest among the branches of the shrubs, and similar in habits and appearance is the garden dormouse that also lives in the taiga and ascends the Alps to 700 m. Two others are present, the forest dormouse and the fat or edible dormouse, the latter being the largest of these squirrel-like rodents, at 18 cm. total length. It is also the most enterprising, ranging across the broad-leaved zone into the mixed forests and southern steppes of Russia and south into the Mediterranean region, although absent from Iberia, except in the extreme north. The fat dormouse is devastating among fruit stores and in orchards. It is the dormouse that was fattened by the Romans, in special containers, for food.

The shrubs and lower branches of the trees feed the large phytophages, the deer, including the roe, fallow and red deer. The fallow has been the sub-

DALTON/NHPA

The common cuckoo is a brood parasite, the hen laying her eggs singly in the nests of small songbirds. A peculiarity of the young cuckoo is that its sibilant call attracts all kinds of small birds, even those carrying back food for their own brood, to fly over and feed it, like the sparrow shown here.

Nuthatch at its nest-hole, with insects for its young. In contrast to the tree creeper it descends the tree head-first as a rule. It eats hazel kernels, wedging a nut in a crevice and hammering with its beak until the shell splits.

Barely 6 cm. long, inclusive of tail, the diminutive common shrew is an habitual insectivore. It hunts insects in the grass or in surface tunnels as well as eating earthworms and carrion. It is little seen in life, but often found dead on bare ground in autumn.

ENGLAND/ARDEA

BEAMES/ARDEA

Far left: Wood mouse, also known as longtailed field mouse, on twig with horse chestnut leaves. This small rodent, the size of a house mouse, occurs in a wide variety of habitats, from dense woodlands to open moors with scattered trees.

Left: The common European mole eating an earthworm, holding it in its front paws. A single mole is reputed to eat its own weight of earthworms in a day, up to 300 worms of mixed sizes. It also eats insect grubs.

Right: Edible dormouse with its litter. Squirrel-like in shape and only slightly smaller than the red squirrel, this dormouse was fattened in special containers by the Romans for the table. Its natural habitat is mature woodland rather than scrub, where smaller species of dormouse are found.

Below, left: Wild boar in a forest clearing with two young. Once common in the deciduous forests of Europe the wild boar can be listed as one of the many predators on the cockchafer, eating them when they fall to the ground.

REINHARD/COLEMAN

ject of so much extermination and re-introduction as to appear almost an alien. At this level and also higher still, even to the topmost branches of the trees, the red squirrel makes a living from the seeds, berries and nuts. Its habit of storing food, not in caches, like the wood mouse, despite the popular belief, but by planting acorns and nuts singly over a wide area, assists the regeneration of the forests.

Inevitably, and completing the food pyramid, the broad-leaved forests are, or were, the home of half a dozen or more carnivores, exploiting the same ecological levels as their prey. On the ground, and also small enough to enter burrows of mice, voles and moles, the weasel pursues its ways. At the surface its larger relatives the polecat and stoat quarter the ground, the stoat often climbing shrubs and trees in pursuit of its prey. As agile among the upper parts of the trees as the squirrels it preys upon is the pine marten, and in places the beech marten, also. The remaining member of the weasel family, the badger, is an omnivore, feeding on worms, slugs, insects and plant foods, and not disdaining carrion.

It used to be thought that there were two species of weasel, the common weasel and the least weasel. It is now set beyond reasonable doubt that there is only one species, the supposed difference being due to a wide variation in size throughout the species' very wide range which includes Europe, North Africa, much of Asia and North America.

In former times there was an abundance of larger carnivores, the wild cat, fox, wolf and lynx, even the brown bear which, although it has a wide diet, is a readily opportunistic carnivore. All these, more so even than the smaller carnivores, have suffered from the destruction of their habitat as well as from active persecution by man. Everywhere in the world the hand of man is against the larger carnivores, not only because of the personal danger they represent but more especially for the threat they pose to man's livestock, from calves and lambs to poultry. This is true also for the winged carnivores—the hawks, eagles, falcons and owls—the most common owl in broad-leaved or mixed forests being the tawny owl.

The lynx illustrates the point well. At one time present throughout the forests and woodlands of Europe, it now has a precarious hold in Scandinavia, Spain and the Balkans. The lynx of southern Europe is more spotted than in Scandinavia and for a long time two species were recognized, a northern lynx and the Spanish lynx. Informed opinion now is that only one species is involved.

Among the winged carnivores, the red kite furnishes probably the most dramatic example of what man can do. Pierre Belon, the French naturalist, writing about 1560, records that there was an amazing number of kites, whether red or black he did not state, collected in the streets of London, eating the refuse thrown into the gutters.

A fallow buck in parkland, the typical present-day home of this deer in many parts of Europe. The distribution of the fallow deer has been so influenced by man for so long, by extermination and re-introduction, that its óriginal range cannot be satisfactorily defined.

The barn owl, found over most of Europe except Scandinavia and Finland, accounts for countless mice, rats and shrews. It avoids thick woodland or wild moorlands, but otherwise has a wide choice of habitat and roosts especially in buildings and in holes in trees or in rocks.

Right: There is probably no more efficient hunter of small rodents than the weasel, which can not only pursue them over the ground but also follow them into their tunnels.

Below, right: Formerly, the lynx ranged from the taiga to the Mediterranean. It was exterminated in the deciduous forest zone long ago, leaving the northern lynx in Scandinavia and the more heavily spotted form, the so-called Spanish lynx, in the Balkans and the Iberian peninsula.

People were forbidden to kill them. The birds were so tame that they fed in the midst of large crowds of people, just as feral pigeons do today. They would even enter butchers' shops and help themselves to meat.

The natural home of the red kite is broad-leaved forests and the edges of forests, preferably wooded river valleys or hilly parklands with damp meadows, or on rocky coasts with trees or scrub. Its natural food is mammals, birds, lizards, frogs, insects, snails and worms. The black kite has a similar but more varied habitat, including areas of fresh water and cultivated land, and more readily frequents towns and villages where it feeds on refuse.

The description of the sixteenth-century scene in London would fit other towns of western Europe until well into the eighteenth century. It

is true for the red kite, to a lesser extent, in the Balearics today, but because of its tendency to kill domestic poultry it has been exterminated over most of Europe. In Wales, for example, the sole remnant of the red kite once widespread over the British Isles has been saved from extinction by the Kite Protection Society.

The black kite, by contrast, is found all over Europe, except for the British Isles and an eastern strip of the Iberian peninsula as well as Holland, which occasionally receives vagrants. It is the most common patrolling raptor along coasts and watercourses, looking for dead and dying fish, and sailing on air currents over broad-leaved and coniferous forests and wooded steppes.

Man is not the only destroyer. Of the many species of animal commonly found in this part of Europe, there are two insects that are worthy of special note for their destructive potential: the cockchafer or Maybug and the gipsy moth. Of the two the cockchafer is the less reviled, because the periods when it is highly damaging are infrequent.

The cockchafer is a large, awkwardly built, brown beetle most commonly seen when it has blundered into a porch light and fallen to the ground to lie helpless on its back, feebly waving its legs. It is abundant from Britain and France to eastern Europe. Its larva lives in the ground, a large white C-shaped grub, feeding on the roots of grasses and especially on those of seedling trees. The adults, which are nocturnal, rest on the leaves of trees by day and feed on them by night and have been known to defoliate a wood.

There have been times when cockchafers have been locally so numerous there were not enough leaves for them to cling to and they have clung to one another, hanging festooned or dropping to the ground in large clusters. In 1574 so many fell into the River Severn in the west of England that they completely clogged the water-wheels of the mills. In 1912, in Austria, 1,000 tonnes were collected by placing receptacles under the trees and beating the branches.

Cockchafers have many enemies, so that plagues such as these seldom occur. Tawny owls, little owls, jays and hawfinches eat them, carnivorous beetles prey on them, and badgers, foxes and wild boars eat them when they fall to the ground. Rooks feed on the grubs, and one pair of jays, observed by a naturalist, fed their babies for 21 days on a total of 20,000 cockchafer grubs.

No doubt, in a large stretch of virgin forest, even a destructive element like the cockchafer has its

ecological function. Local defoliation would do little to diminish the climacteric value of the forest but would produce dead wood so necessary for other species. An example might be the stag beetle, another large beetle found over the same range as the cockchafer but with a very patchy distribution. In the British Isles, for example, it is found only in a belt south of London. Its larvae feed for several years in rotten stumps and dead trees before changing to the adult. With modern "clean" forestry in Europe, the stag beetle is much more rare than formerly.

Wherever it occurs in the deciduous forest the larvae of the gipsy moth cause devastation by devouring the leaves of the trees and shrubs. This moth is common throughout Europe, although absent from the British Isles. The male is dark brown, the female white and larger, and although her wings are fully developed she does not fly. It is difficult therefore to understand how the gipsy moth spreads so widely. The secret is that the very young caterpillars are covered with long, fine hairs and readily become wind-borne like thistledown or gossamer spiders. As they are not particular what kind of leaves they eat, wherever they happen to come down they find plenty of food.

DALTON/NHPA

Adult cockchafers feed on leaves of trees and plants, and may cause serious damage. On occasions they have been seen hanging in clusters on foliage, like swarms of giant bees. Fortunately their many enemies help to control their numbers.

BISSEROT/COLEMAN

A pair of stag beetles, the male with his large 'antlers'. Stag beetle larvae feed for several years in rotten tree trunks and stumps, acting as one of the primary agents in returning their substance to the soil.

Below, left: The red kite, distinguished by its long, deeply forked chestnut tail, preys on small birds and on mammals up to the size of a rabbit. It readily takes carrion and was once a welcome scavenger in the streets of large towns.

The more common black kite is also a natural scavenger but is more gregarious than the red kite. It lives near lakes and rivers, where there are woods or scattered trees, except in the southern and eastern parts of Europe, where it lives near villages.

Wherever it occurs the gypsy moth, the female of which is shown here, is a potential destroyer of the foliage of trees. The caterpillars cause the damage, readily becoming windborne to reach new supplies of food.

REINHARD/COLEMAN

ZEPF/NHPA

Don mares and foals, domesticated horses, on the Russian steppes where once the herds of tarpan, Europe's now extinct wild horse, grazed in herds.

The Steppes

The steppes, a name of Russian origin, denote more particularly the extensive plains of north-west Asia. These extend, however, into south-east Europe, to the region north of the Black Sea, and are referred to here purely for convenience as the Russian steppes. Similar terrain is found beyond the Carpathians, where it is more usually spoken of as the Plains of Hungary. Steppes are the counterpart of the North American prairies and the savannahs elsewhere, a vast area of undulating grassland.

The Russian steppes have changed less than any other part of Europe during and subsequent to the ice ages. During the ice ages the steppes formed part of the tundra bordering the southern limit of the ice cap. After the ice cap had receded the formation of forests was inhibited by the cold winters, minimal rainfall and hot, dry summers. Wind and sun play uninterrupted across these plains and temperature and humidity vary enormously between night and day. A large part of central Europe also became steppe following the last ice age, but there the climate allowed the development of climax forests.

Until the beginning of the present century the Russian steppes were largely covered with vast expanses, as far as the horizon, of grasses, especially feathergrasses, and low flowering herbs, an area marvellously changing with successive seasons of the year. Over these plains roamed herds of wild horses, sometimes bison, and the saiga antelope. Smaller animals, living among the herbage, the sousliks, voles and mice, were protected by the vegetation from the heat of the sun or the cold winds, and either lived under the snow or hibernated during the bitter winters. All but the saiga, among the hoofed animals, are gone. The tarpan, the European wild horse, formerly widespread over central Europe, became extinct in the wild in 1851, the last being killed in the Ukraine. A small remnant of the bison has been preserved in the Bielowecza forest in Poland. The steppes were also the home of ground birds like the bustard, partridge, larks, pipits and wheatears, with insect-eating falcons, the hobby, kestrel, lesser kestrel and saker, and marsh harriers as the chief birds of prey.

The steppes are not uniform. A semi-desert area extending around the Caspian Sea was covered by salt water during the last stages of the ice ages. The ground is salty and the vegetation mainly the salt-loving wormwood (Artemisia). Beyond this is the grassy steppe of the Ukraine and beyond this

Kestrel on a post with red-berried briar beside it. The scene is more typical of western Europe, but the kestrel is found throughout Europe, even on the steppes, to which its slightly smaller, noisier and more gregarious relative, the lesser kestrel is confined.

the forest steppe where the grassland becomes more and more dotted with trees to merge insensibly into the forests of northern Russia. Even on the steppes proper there are islands of higher ground where some trees are growing, and these are richer in animal life than the surrounding flatter land, but even there the numbers of species are limited.

The desert steppes may have sand or clay soil and on the former live gerbils, the northern three-toed jerboa, Eversmann's hamster, feeding on the long roots of the semi-desert plants, and the long-eared hedgehog. Among the predators on these are the wolf, steppe and marbled polecats, and the

BURTON/COLEMAN

Sousliks are ground squirrels, and lack the bushy tail of the tree squirrel. There are two species, the European souslik of eastern to south-eastern Europe and the spotted souslik farther east, confined to the steppes.

Right: The common polecat ranges over nearly all of Europe except the north, the Balkans and the larger Mediterranean islands. Its relative, the marbled polecat is confined to the steppes area, and is only found in patches even there.

corsac fox. Among the few birds is the shore lark, a bird found in many kinds of habitat elsewhere, and which runs along the ground chasing flying insects as they dance over the dry ground.

There are more plants growing on the clay steppe, giving more food and better protection for small animals, the commonest of which are the sousliks. These are ground squirrels and they hibernate in their burrows for eight months of the year, packing all their activities such as breeding and laying in fat for hibernation into a space of four months. There are several kinds of short-toed and calandra larks as well as sandgrouse, the latter being remarkable for their long daily flights

BURTON/COLEMAN

in search of water. Flocks of houbara bustard search for insects, snails and lizards as well as plant food, and the tawny eagle, the chief predator of the clay steppe, hunts the sousliks and the larks, as well as taking carrion and frogs.

The largest animal on the dry steppe is the saiga, the strange-looking antelope with a dramatic history, easily recognized by its curious muzzle, prolonged as a short trunk, and its amber-coloured horns. It also lives on the Asiatic steppes and it once ranged, during the historical period, to the Carpathians and, until the eighteenth century, to southern Poland. Remains of the saiga have been found in Solutrean deposits of England and in parts of western France.

There were fears that the saiga might become extinct in the 1930s, after a succession of severe winters and because of hunting, although it had been protected by law since 1919. Only a few hundred were left. Then came a resurgence, and by 1960 the total population reached two million of which a quarter were living between the Volga and Ural rivers, where an annual cull of 150,000 to 200,000 beasts provided 6,000 tonnes of meat and 186,000 square metres of hides.

The steppes proper, represented by the Ukraine, and extending beyond the Carpathians as the Plains of Hungary, are sometimes referred to as the "steppe corridor", and are a continuation of the Asiatic steppes into Europe. It was the corridor through which successive invaders—Huns, Goths and Visigoths—swarmed into Europe. These flat plains were covered with feathergrass, from knee-height to shoulder-height, spangled with red tulips and anemones, followed by dwarf iris and fernleaf peonies, thistles and larkspur in spring. In early summer patches of blue sage interspersed the grasses which in late summer turned the steppes into a sea of silver, when the feathergrasses bloomed. After this the steppe became an area of dust as the vegetation, baked by the heat of summer, was broken up. Later in the year, just before the first snows in November, the shoots of fresh grass turned the steppes into a vast sheet of emerald green.

During the second half of the nineteenth century the Ukraine became a great industrial area, based on rich deposits of iron, coal and other materials. It also supported herds of cattle, sheep, goats and pigs. Above all, it has become a great agricultural area, its topsoil a thick layer of fertile black earth, ideal for growing grain.

A rich fertile earth is characteristic of deciduous forests, and primitive agriculture consisted of burning the forests to create agricultural land. On the steppes there has been no destruction of forests. The climax vegetation was not achieved. Instead, they reached the stage of grasslands only, supporting in former times vast numbers of hoofed animals, including the now extinct aurochs, the almost extinct bison, red and roe deer, the extinct wild horse and the saiga. These were the large "converters", turning grasses into fertilizing dung, their carcasses feeding the predators, including the wolf, and scavengers such as the kite. The steppes were probably their summer home from which they migrated to the forests for the winter. Most of them are now found in forested regions as well, but their populations were most dense on the steppes. The accumulation over thousands of years of dead or converted grasses and other herbage, and the waste and bodies of large numbers of animals, from rodents to the mighty aurochs, would be sufficient to account for the legacy of proverbially rich black earth, known as chernozem, although it is hard to say what influence extinct herds may have had on the soil. At least the soil would not have needed artificial fertilizers.

Alpine marmot gathering hay in preparation for winter hibernation. Its relative, the bobak or steppe marmot, is a characteristic animal of the steppes, but is virtually extinct in the rest of Europe.

Left: The saiga, Europe's only antelope, is the largest animal on the dry steppe. In the 1930s it approached the edge of extinction, but it has now enjoyed a resurgence.

A typical steppe scene in southern Russia, with sheep of the new Askaniya breed grazing on a seemingly endless plain.

COLEMAN

Large as a turkey, a poor flyer but a good runner, the bustard is particularly well represented on the steppes and on a few other plains in Europe. It is a vagrant elsewhere but being a good target for the marksman has been badly persecuted.

The ubiquitous red fox is one of several predators on the many small mammals that flourish on the grasslands of the virgin steppes. It is not always realized how significant is its role, there and elsewhere, in controlling the numbers of mice and rats.

The bobak or steppe marmot, 55 cm. long, uniformly brown except for the dark brown tip to the tail, is the characteristic steppe animal. In Siberia today its grass-covered mounds up to 1 m. high cover the ground, 30–40 to a hectare. It has been unable to adapt to cultivation and is virtually extinct in Europe, even in the reserves. The souslik or spotted ground squirrel, 25 cm. long with tail 5 cm. long, dark brown with white spots, has survived. It is a natural cultivator, turning just over a cubic metre of soil per hectare each year. The souslik is the favourite food of the black kite, a common bird on the steppes, which also feeds on other rodents as well as carrion and insects. The black kite usually detects the souslik while soaring in the air, but it can also hover like a kestrel or fly very low, like a harrier, a metre or so above the ground, in order to take its prey by surprise. Sometimes the bird flies in pursuit of a running souslik, or sits in watch beside the burrows of these rodents.

Grasslands are a paradise for small mammals and the virgin steppes abound in mice, including field mice, harvest mice and the longtailed field mice, as well as the common and pygmy shrews. In addition there are the jerboas, the so-called jump-

REINHARD/COLEMAN

Another controller of small mammals that has suffered at the hands of man is the stoat. Its natural range is the whole of Europe, including the steppes, but it is now virtually absent from the whole of the Mediterranean region.

The common hamster is the largest of the hamsters, in size and proportions more like a guinea pig, but with a short tail. It is discontinuously distributed over central Europe but is more abundantly found on the steppes.

ing rats, especially the great jerboa, as well as the common and grey hamsters and several dormice, including the edible or fat dormouse. Their natural predators are fox, stoat, weasel and polecat. Birds typical of steppes are the larks and pipits and the great and little bustard. A visitor from Africa is the demoiselle crane, which feeds on slugs, snails, lizards and snakes.

On the Russian steppes the lizards are the steppe and sand lizards and the snakes include the whipsnake and the four-lined snake. Frogs are few. Where water is available the edible frog breeds, and the typical amphibian is the variegated toad. The most prominent insect is the migratory locust, its swarms followed especially by the rose-coloured starling or rosy pastor and the lesser kestrel, but as always where locusts abound they provide food for numbers of birds and beasts.

To the north of the steppes, and lying between them and the broad-leaved forests of the north, a wide transitional belt of wooded steppe runs right across Russia. It is a region of more undulating country where steppe and forest alternate and illustrates what takes place in the succession from one to the other. It also indicates what much of Europe must have looked like as the ice cap finally

The stronghold of the common crane is the wet ground of northern Europe, south-eastwards to the Russian steppes, but it is found also in parts of Yugoslavia. Cranes cause some damage to crops, but help to keep down populations of wireworms and other insect larvae, which they take from the soil with their long beaks.

79

The woodpigeon, recognizable by its white 'collar', drinking. Pigeons are unusual among birds in not raising the head to swallow water.

Montagu's harrier alighting. These long-legged hawks, superb as aerial acrobats during the breeding season, are found across central Europe, from England and Iberia to the Urals, on marshes, fens, moors and cultivated land.

BISSEROT/COLEMAN

The migratory locust, the scourge of the hotter parts of the Old World, has managed to penetrate into the Russian steppes. Sometimes it appears in large numbers, when the lesser kestrels converge on the swarms as they do in Africa in winter.

Left: The broad, rounded wings and long tail of the sparrowhawk give it high manoeuvrability for the pursuit of small birds through the woods. This same manoeuvrability is useful in other kinds of country. As a result, except where it has been deliberately exterminated, this common hawk may be found anywhere in Europe.

The buzzard's prey is small mammals, up to the size of rabbits, and insects, rarely small birds. It nests on rocky ledges, in trees or on the ground on rocky coasts, plains, moors and mountain slopes, virtually throughout Europe.

REINHARD/COLEMAN

receded and before more or less continuous forest had taken over. In places the ground is pock-marked with rounded depressions, often filled with water, up to 45 m. across and down to 2 m. deep, a reminder of the pools left everywhere by the melting ice. The number of plants and animals increases rapidly in the wooded steppes, the animals using the trees for shelter and coming out on to the grasslands to feed.

At the southernmost limit of the wooded steppe the grassland is merely broken by clumps of trees or small forests, mostly of the common peduncu-late oak. As one travels north the wooded areas increase to give open oakwoods, often of large extent, each surrounded by steppe and itself broken by open glades carpeted with low flowering plants. At the same time the woods become increasingly mixed, with smooth-leaved elms, birches, com-mon and Norway maples, lime, aspen and hazel. The post-glacial crater-like depressions may con-tain sallow and dewberry, while raspberry thickets alternate with beds of nettles up to two metres high. Sometimes the forest encloses an area of steppe, in which the characteristic bird is the yellowhammer.

Wooded steppe is alive with fox, badger and roe deer, and the elk is sometimes seen there although it is more an inhabitant of the taiga. The larks and pipits are joined by whinchats, blackcaps, serins, great tits, blackbirds, thrushes, goldfinches, lin-nets, and hawfinches. Tree sparrows are there in large numbers, also the common robin, with wood pigeons and woodpeckers, the turtle dove and stock dove. The raptors include, in addition to the black kite, the sparrowhawk and the honey buzzard, Montagu's harrier and the pallid harrier not found elsewhere in Europe. There are also more amphibians and reptiles in the forests of the wooded steppe. They include a spadefoot toad, the field frog, slow worm, sand lizard, steppe viper and variegated toad.

Although the Russian steppes lie roughly be-tween latitudes 45°N and 55°N, with their south-ern limit north of the sub-tropical Mediterranean region, there is an area on the north-west shore of the Black Sea with a permanent breeding ground of the migratory locust, the species more typical of Africa and the Middle East. From this area, at irregular intervals, swarms migrate in a north-erly direction and also north-west and west into central Europe. Occasionally Black Sea locusts reach the British Isles, even as far north as the Orkney and Shetland Islands.

The Mediterranean Maquis

The Mediterranean region embraces three European peninsulas projecting into the Mediterranean Sea, with numerous associated islands. It includes the Iberian peninsula, the south of France, Italy and the Balkans. It represents that part of Europe which escaped the main ravages of the ice cap that spread south over the continent during successive ice ages. Nevertheless, along its northern border are the Swiss Alps which have their own glaciation even today. This was probably more extensive still during the early part of the last 25,000 years, the period that has elapsed since the end of the last Ice Age.

The climate of the Mediterranean region is subtropical, with winter rains and summer sunshine, and the spring of each year sees a riot of colourful flowers. It is a congenial region that has become a holiday area for the rest of Europe. These same propitious circumstances led to its early colonization by man, resulting in its becoming the cradle of western civilization. From this early Arcadia it has become the most ravaged, biologically, of all Europe.

There is evidence that the abundance enjoyed by Ancient Greece was thrown away by misuse of the land. The forests were exploited for their timber and this, together with the keeping of herds of sheep and goats, which devastated the vegetation, induced soil erosion and loss of agricultural productivity, leading to the decline of the early Greek culture. In place of mountains covered with forests of broad-leaved trees and, above these, forests of conifers, the mountains are now deserts and the vegetation on the lower slopes and on the lowlands is reduced mainly to shrubs and low evergreen trees. This is the maquis, or macchia, vegetation.

Following the decline of Greece, the Roman Empire dominated. The Romans were guilty of the same misuse of the land and were compelled, by conquest, to extend their boundaries to provide a larder for Rome. The Roman Empire lasted longer than the period of Greek culture but the end was the same. The Iberian peninsula fared no better, and the prophets of gloom, viewing the continued mismanagement of land resources even today, predict total disaster in the end for the Mediterranean region if nothing is done to reverse the process.

All this represents a catastrophic spoliation of the habitat, which has had a dramatic effect on the fauna. Within the last few years, oceanographers have become alarmed also at the condi-

BURTON

tion of the Mediterranean Sea itself, which is becoming heavily polluted with sewage, especially around the holiday beaches.

Such is the buoyancy of nature, even within this gloomy setting, that there is still a diversity of animals worthy of study, although man over the centuries has done his best to eradicate them. It would be surprising if it were otherwise. In all parts of the world, in passing from pole to equator, the animals become more numerous as to species and more colourful in appearance. The same is true for that part of the spectrum from the arctic coastline of Europe to the northern shores of the Mediterranean. It is true more especially of the birds and for two reasons particularly. The first is that many birds more typical of the African avifauna are permanently resident in countries along the northern shore of the Mediterranean. The second is that some species of colourful birds migrate from Africa each summer, into Mediterranean Europe. Some, in fact, move northwards beyond the maquis.

It would perhaps have been more correct to say that this is how the Mediterranean region ought to be, and would be but for man's interference. As it is, the sierras of Spain, the Apennines in Italy and the mountains of Greece are largely denuded of vegetation and eroded of soil, which has been washed into valleys where the soil is already fertile and the maquis flourishes, except where the valleys have been taken over for agriculture. Compared with the rest of Europe, there has been, at least in the past and to a large extent still, relatively little respect for wildlife. Any bird the size of a starling or larger is likely to be shot. Efforts are being made

Previous page: Golden oriole with its nest. The bird was named for its flute-like call, *orr-i-ole*, but its noisy cat-like call, harsh as the common jay's, is easier to hear, and makes it easier to locate. Although outstandingly coloured it is not easy to see because of its skulking habits.

Left: The villain of the piece, flocks of goats in northern Greece. In other parts of the world there is unimpeachable evidence of the goat's ability to reduce a floral paradise to an arid desert. There is reason to believe that the spoilt landscape of the Mediterranean region is due to the same cause.

Right: Man has outstripped the animal in maltreating his environment, culminating in the twentieth century nightmare of pollution, as on this oil-polluted beach at Algarve, Portugal.

An aerial view of a scrub-covered landscape in Greece, with the red earth intersected by paths, possibly worn by goats. It is a fair guess that this area was once covered with luxuriant vegetation.

The bee-eater flies swallow-like with quick wing-beats as it circles to swoop on bees, wasps, flies, beetles and dragonflies. Brilliantly coloured, it is distinguished by the long thin bill and the long central tail feathers.

Whether its crest is spread or folded, the pinkish-brown hoopoe, with its black-and-white wings can hardly be confused with any other bird. Hoopoes feed mainly on the ground, taking grubs, insects and worms with their long, curved bills.

to alter this by setting aside as reserves those places where songbirds congregate, especially where they rest on migration.

A high percentage of the birds listed for countries of central and western Europe are summer visitors. They make their way from Africa in spring and return in autumn along three main flyways. One is down the Iberian peninsula to cross the sea at the Strait of Gibraltar. Another is down the length of Italy, to Sicily, and thence to Tunisia. The third flyway, in the eastern Mediterranean, has a dual character: the birds may fly down across the central Balkans, or across the eastern Balkans and Asia Minor, both routes continuing along the Nile Valley once Africa is reached; some species may use one route when flying north and the other when flying south.

In effect, these are three corridors used by summer visitors to the rest of Europe, and it is unfortunate for the rest of Europe that the migrants should be netted and shot in large numbers when en route or in places where they touch down to rest. This has long been a matter of international concern among ornithologists.

Apart from the Spanish Marismas and the Camargue, the occasional thickets of uninterrupted maquis in undisturbed fertile valleys give us the clearest indication of what the Mediterranean avifauna must have been like in the past. It has been said that the song of the warblers in such places is almost deafening. Warblers are among the smallest of the songbirds and are not conspicuous for their colouring, being mainly shades of brown, olive green, and yellow. In their songs they are persistent and melodious, some of them pouring forth their liquid notes in a cascade of sound. It is not so much that the warblers are more numerous in this region as that there is a greater number of species, about twice as many as in other regions of Europe.

To the melody of the warblers can be added the colours of the hoopoes, bee-eaters and rollers, the finches, buntings and rock thrushes. Before the vegetation was ravaged and the practice of hunting small birds was developed, the whole Mediterranean region must have been truly Arcadian.

It is, however, difficult to generalize, for southern Europe is, in effect, composed of three regions, each a peninsula jutting into the sea and each diverse in its flora and fauna while all three retain features in common. The diversity can best be illustrated by reference to the species of sparrows, of which there are five. The common house

FERNANDEZ/COLEMAN

Griffon vultures feed on the decaying carcasses of large animals. These it used to find, in many parts of Europe, left unburied. With the spread of regulations for the disposal of dead livestock the range and numbers of the vulture in southern Europe are dwindling.

No bird anywhere in the world has more completely attached itself to human dwellings than the house sparrow, yet some of its fellows still nest in bushes in open country, in hedges, in trees and among rocks.

BEVAN/ARDEA

sparrow is found throughout the region, except in Italy and the islands of Sicily, Sardinia and Corsica. The tree sparrow has the same wide range except for the Balkans, Sardinia and Corsica. The rock sparrow is everywhere except in the extreme north of Italy and the northern Balkans. The Spanish sparrow is found over most of Spain, in Sardinia, Sicily, southern Italy and the Balkans. The Italian sparrow is found only in Italy and Corsica.

Birds of prey, although affected by the destruction of the habitat, and with this the loss or reduction of prey species, as well as by persecution, are nevertheless a conspicuous feature of the region, as compared with the rest of Europe. In addition to the presence of many of the birds of prey found in other parts of Europe, Mediterranean Europe affords hospitality to the Egyptian vulture, the griffon vulture, the black vulture, the bearded vulture or lammergeier, the imperial eagle, Bonelli's eagle, and the booted eagle.

As with the sparrows, the birds of prey are not ranged throughout the region. The Egyptian

87

vulture is found more or less throughout, the griffon vulture discontinuously, but mainly in Spain and the Balkans, while the black vulture is found in Spain and the Balkans and also in Sicily and Sardinia. Bonelli's eagle is discontinuous throughout and the booted eagle is confined to Spain and the Balkans.

Whether it is the nature of the terrain or persecution that has dictated the vagaries of the distribution of the birds of prey, is a complex question which cannot be discussed here. A possible clue may be found in the history of the bearded vulture, the lammergeier or "lamb-eagle" as it is alternatively known. A carrion-eater by habit, it has the reputation of stealing lambs, which is either wholly unfounded or only partially deserved. Whatever the truth, this mag-

nificent raptor, that descends from its mountain eyrie to scavenge the plains, looks like a huge falcon with its long pointed wings and diamond-shaped tail.

Perhaps its appearance was its undoing, both its large size and its falcon-like shape. At all events, it has been shot out of parts of its range. The last breeding lammergeier in Bavaria was killed in 1835, in the Swiss Alps the last was shot in 1826, and in the Carpathians the last was killed with poisoned bait in 1935. Occasionally one wanders farther north from its present range, which is from Spain to the Balkans, including Corsica, Sardinia and Sicily.

The presence of these African species of vultures and eagles in Mediterranean Europe as well as of other, smaller birds more typical of Africa, recalls

The ruin lizard *Lacerta sicula* is found in large numbers in many parts of the Mediterranean area, especially in Italy and on neighbouring islands. Altogether 21 subspecies have been named.

Left: The lammergeier or bearded vulture at its nest high up in the mountains. The nest is typically an untidy structure made up of all manner of refuse, such as rotting bones, pieces of skin and fragments of tortoises, all the remains of the bird's meals, with a few slender branches and other plant material added.

The poisonous adder is easily recognized by the bold black zigzag line down its back and a black V or X on the head. Its colour is variable, even to nearly black, which tends to obscure the well-known danger warnings on its head and back.

that the region has many other links with Africa. During the Mesozoic era, which ended about 70 million years ago, what is now the Mediterranean Sea was part of a much larger sea, known as the Tethys Sea, which extended eastwards to the Indo-Pacific. This severed the Eurasian continent from Africa. The levels of the bed of the Tethys Sea have varied, as well as its extent; at times during the Tertiary era, especially during the Oligocene, there appear to have been land-bridges from Africa to southern Europe.

Although study of these possible land-bridges is still proceeding, that they must have existed seems beyond doubt, judging from the reptiles and amphibians presently found in Mediterranean Europe. These two classes of cold-blooded land vertebrates are represented by numerous species in the tropics and sub-tropics. The numbers of species decrease sharply in the temperate regions. In Europe the reptile that goes farthest north is the adder, and this is not found much beyond the southern limit of the taiga. An amphibian, the common or grass frog, *Rana temporaria*, goes farther north, to just north of the Arctic Circle. The numbers increase as we go south, but nowhere in Europe, north of the Mediterranean region, is there any more than a handful of species, usually six at the most, in any one region.

The Mediterranean region has twenty-nine amphibians and seventy-eight reptiles. These include several species typical of Africa. Because of the generally milder climate, this abundance is to be expected, but some of the types present, especially of reptiles, are an indication that there must have been land-bridges at one time where the

The harmless grass snake, or water snake, of Europe usually lives on low-lying, often damp ground and hunts its prey (primarily frogs and toads) in the water.

The common or viviparous lizard is widespread across Europe, in the lowlands and highlands, in sand dunes, woods, meadows and marshes. The young are born so far developed that they tear through the membrane of the egg either as it is being laid or soon after.

Strait of Gibraltar is now, between Tunisia, Sicily and Italy, and from north-east Africa to the Balkans. The seventy-eight reptiles include four geckos, a chameleon, thirty-nine lizards, twenty-seven snakes, two terrapins, a pond tortoise and four land tortoises. The amphibians include thirteen newts and salamanders and sixteen frogs and toads. Several of the lizards have probably been introduced, possibly accidentally in ships' cargoes. If so, it would have been a long time ago, and even if these must be excluded as aliens it still leaves a formidable list of species by European standards.

Three of the species of lizards offer an interesting example of the formation of sub-species due to isolation on islands. There has been a similar subspeciation in voles on small islands around Great Britain, and recent studies suggest that their ancestors reached the islands in cargoes of fodder landed there from coracles in the days before the Roman Conquest, two thousand years ago. The Mediterranean lizards have probably a longer history of subspeciation. For example, the lizard *Lacerta sicula* is divided into thirty-nine sub-species, *L. pityuensis* into thirty-two and *L. erhardi* into thirty-one. Some of these may have reached their present location naturally, but it cannot be ruled out that others may have been taken there accidentally or deliberately (for example, as pets) by man. This is only one of many indications which suggest that the present-day craze for keeping pets is as old as the hills—or at least as old as some of the early domestications of animals.

Reptiles generally tend to flourish in dry, sunny habitats, and since most of them are insect-eaters the loss of vegetation cover in the Mediterranean region is less of a disadvantage than it would be to some other animal types. A striking adaptation is shown by some races of the lizard *Lacerta melisellensis* living on rocky islands in the Adriatic. They live especially among colonies of breeding gulls and feed on the lice and mites that infest the gulls and their nests.

Pet-keeping can not only add to a fauna but also

The eyed lizard, the finest and most colourful of European lizards, has a tail that accounts for two-thirds of its length. Because of its size, it is able to take larger prey than some other species, prey which includes mice, other lizards and snakes.

The Iberian or spur-thighed tortoise with eggs. In the wild it eats rotting parts of plants and dead animals. As a garden tortoise it should be given equivalent foods and prevented from reaching garden seedlings, which it enjoys even more.

subtract from it, and a prime example is seen in the land tortoises of southern Europe. There are three: the Iberian or Algerian tortoise, misleadingly named *Testudo graeca*, of north-west Africa, Spain and the northern Balkans, as well as Iraq and Iran; the Greek or Hermann's tortoise, *T. hermanni*, of the Balkans (other than Greece), Italy, southern France and some of the Mediterranean islands; and the margined tortoise *T. marginata* of southern Greece and Sardinia (where it was introduced by soldiers during World War II). *Testudo graeca* is also called the Garden Tortoise and is the one that has been kept as a pet in gardens for centuries. The famous Timothy, mentioned by Gilbert White, the eighteenth-century English naturalist, that lived for 54 years, belonged to this species.

For the past few decades thousands of Iberian tortoises have been exported each year for sale as pets, a practice that often results in high mortalities in transit. It has been observed in Greece, after a fire has destroyed undergrowth, that the ground may be littered with a surprising number of shells of dead tortoises, mainly small ones. Even if the Iberian tortoise existed in such numbers it would be surprising if its capture for the pet trade has not

Common hedgehog with the berries of the wild arum. It is sometimes supposed that this animal eats only insects, slugs, snails and earthworms. There is now reason to believe that at least some fruit is eaten, the kind of fruit varying with the individual.

A female Barbary ape with her baby on her back. This species of monkey is native to north-west Africa and has found its way to Gibraltar, probably taken there by man in a semi-domesticated state.

Previous page: The Scottish wild cat is a subspecies of the European wild cat. It was once widespread over Britain but is now found only in the Highlands of Scotland.

A tropical type of insect found throughout the Mediterranean region is the scarab, sacred to the Ancient Egyptians from its habit of trundling a ball of dung: the insects were accepted as symbolic of the force that keeps the Earth revolving.

DALTON/NHPA

Ant-lions are more associated with tropical regions than with Europe, but are in fact common in Mediterranean areas. One species reaches as far north as southern Sweden. Adults are less well-known than their larvae, whose predatory habits have given the animal its name.

BURTON/COLEMAN

Ant-lion larvae trap their prey in pits which they dig in sandy soil. The larva waits in the pit until a passing insect falls in, then seizes it with its large, pincer-like jaws.

made serious inroads to the point where a natural catastrophe could eliminate it over a wide part of its range.

Although there are six mammals living in Mediterranean Europe that at first sight appear to have come from Africa, present-day opinion is that only one arrived there naturally. The genet *Genetta genetta*, widespread throughout the savannah of Africa, as well as in North Africa, has long been living in Iberia and southern France. It belongs to the same family (Viverridae) as the mongoose, although it looks like a slender tabby cat. It has been long established in south-west Europe and once extended as far north as Belgium and into Germany. Being a small carnivore, it probably there came into competition with martens, which may be why it died out in these more northern parts. There should be no reason why the genet may not be regarded as a natural invader from Africa, as the Mediterranean region lacks martens and the stoat. Nevertheless, the Roman authors referred to plagues of rabbits in Iberia, and the genet may have been introduced by the Romans to counter the rabbit.

The Egyptian mongoose *Herpestes ichneumon* has a similar distribution, except that in Europe it is confined to Iberia, where it also was probably introduced by the Romans.

The Algerian hedgehog *Erinaceus algirus* is found on the Balearic islands and in a few localities on the Mediterranean coasts of Spain and France. At least one eminent zoologist has suggested it is a relic from Pliocene times, but the greater probability is that the Algerian hedgehog is in Europe because it was once popular as a pet. Hedgehogs have been favourite pets since Roman times, possibly earlier, and may well have been imported.

On Gibraltar live a few Barbary apes, *Macaca sylvana*, pets of the British garrison, and so domesticated that, especially in view of their vernacular name, there can be little doubt they were taken there from Africa.

Another African animal is the crested porcupine *Hystrix cristata*. It is found in Sicily and Italy, and more recently it has been introduced into Albania and thence to Yugoslavia. Its real home is the northern half of Africa and present-day informed opinion inclines to the view that the porcupines in Europe are descendants of animals taken to Italy—possibly as pets?

This leaves only the jackal, *Canis aureus*, living in the Balkans, but since it ranges over Asia and

Africa it can be reasonably accepted as a natural invader from Asia.

A discussion of these (presumably) exotic mammals has an importance in another field. The household cat was probably domesticated in Egypt, almost certainly from the bush cat *Felis lybica*. This is found over virtually the whole of Africa, but it is also found in south-west Asia, from Arabia to Turkestan and northern India. One leading authority has also identified the wild cat living in Corsica, Sardinia and Sicily as *F. lybica*.

The bush cat, the wild cat of Europe, *F. silvestris*, and its sub-species the Scottish wild cat, *F. s. grampia*, are all so alike in appearance that it is virtually impossible to separate them. They are all three alike in behaviour, including their psychology, and opinion is hardening to the view that they are indeed one species. That being so, it becomes a matter for speculation whether the wild cat reached Europe from Africa or from Asia, or both. Whichever way it is decided, the wild cat has more thoroughly colonized Europe than any invader, from south or east, other than the house mouse or the two rats, and it did so before either of these arrived.

Taking everything into consideration it would seem that any invasion by African animals across land-bridges must have taken place early, that is, before present-day species of mammals had evolved. These bridges would have let across the reptiles and also some of the lower animals such as scorpions as well as insects such as the ant-lion, which are a feature of parts of the Mediterranean region.

The adult ant-lion bears some resemblance to a

Above, right: Six-spot burnet moth on field scabious. The brilliant and conspicuous colours of the moth are warning colours, indicating that it has an unpleasant taste. Any bird taking such a moth in its beak soon rejects it and never touches its like again.

Right: The song of the cicada, typical of the tropical night, is heard also in Mediterranean Europe. One species, *Cicadetta montana*, extends as far north as Sweden, and is also found in the New Forest, in the extreme south of England.

Red admiral butterfly, one of the larger butterflies of Europe, famous for its bright colouring and for the extensive migrations it makes northwards (and possibly southwards in return).

FLETCHER/NSP

dragonfly. The typical European species, *Myrmeleon formicarius*, is about 25 mm. long with two pairs of gauzy wings spanning 50 mm. when spread. It is, however, the larva that gives the vernacular name. This has a short, thick, fleshy body with a disproportionately large pair of jaws. The larva digs a conical pit 50 mm. deep and 75 mm. across in sandy soil, at the bottom of which it lies in wait for any insect stumbling into the pit. It will help an insect to fall in by disturbing the sand on the side of the pit, or even flick sand at an insect hesitating on the brink, making it slide down.

In parts of tropical Africa, where the soil is sandy, groups of these pits are a feature of the microlandscape. Some of the African adult ant-lions are 75 mm. long and the pits are correspondingly large and conspicuous. Similar but smaller groups are a feature of the sandy soil of the Mediterranean region, in the south of France, for example.

A useful and attractive insect, the sacred scarab beetle, also lives in the Mediterranean region of Europe. It is more commonly linked with Ancient Egypt where it was deified, but its European members were also made famous by the French entomologist Jean Henri Fabre. This is the beetle, 30 mm. long, which makes a ball of cattle or goat's dung as big as a man's fist and rolls it along the ground, pushing it backwards with its hind legs. Two scarabs may share the task of trundling the ball, and they may be of the same sex. They roll it to a suitable spot, then bury it and feed on it underground until it is finished. Then they collect another ball. Towards the end of summer a pair, male and female, team up to bury a ball of dung, but now an underground chamber is prepared for it and the female shreds it and remoulds it into the shape of a pear. In the narrow neck of the pear she makes a small cavity and in this lays an egg. The larva hatching from the egg lives on the store of food and emerges as a beetle in the following spring.

A large and distinctive group of moths, the burnet moths, genus *Zygaena*, has its centre of distribution around the coasts of the Mediterranean, both European and North African, and westwards into Asia Minor. From this area the species decrease rapidly in all directions. There are around four dozen species in southern Europe and the number drops to seven in Denmark and Britain and to only two in the extreme north. All the burnets are brightly coloured moths that fly slowly in the sun but are more commonly seen on flowers in meadows. Birds leave them alone, although the moths are

conspicuous, because they give out a poisonous fluid when disturbed, and a bird that has once taken a burnet in its bill will not do so again. It recognizes from its colouring that the insect should be avoided.

Most insects stay more or less where they are hatched. Some winged species and a few wingless species may be widely dispersed by the wind, but as a whole insects are sedentary. There are, however, a fair number which are known to make seasonal migrations, resembling the better-known migrations of birds. There is, however, a difference. Most of the insects appear to fly only northwards in the spring and summer without a corresponding southward return as winter approaches.

The best-documented migrations are those which take place between the Mediterranean region and northern Europe, including the British Isles. A number of familiar butterflies and moths, and others less familiar to people living in the latitudes of Britain, Holland and Denmark, cannot survive the winter in any of their stages. They breed in North Africa and southern Europe and, for reasons so far not discovered, they fly northwards in the early summer. The red admiral is one of Britain's most familiar butterflies, but all those seen in late summer on Michaelmas daisies are the offspring of parents which flew in across the English Channel earlier in the year. There is some evidence that these autumn butterflies fly south again, but it is not known whether they ever reach areas where they can survive and breed during the winter.

The silver Y moth is comparable to the red admiral, but it both migrates and breeds in large numbers. Illuminated moth traps in England sometimes capture hundreds in a single night.

The most celebrated of these migrant butterflies is the painted lady. Great swarms of them have been seen taking off from their breeding grounds in North Africa, in semi-desert areas, and flying northwards. This butterfly is such a compulsive migrant that it has spread all over the habitable world and is frequently seen within the Arctic Circle.

The largest single swarm of the painted lady was recorded in California in 1924 and was estimated at 3,000 million individuals. An earlier record, for Switzerland, in 1826, was said to form a belt 3 m. wide which took two hours to pass.

The clouded yellow and Bath white butterflies behave in a similar way but only fly north in any appreciable numbers at long intervals of years. For example, both butterflies reached England in quantity in 1947, and a few clouded yellows are recorded every year, but the Bath white has hardly been seen since 1947.

Some of the large hawk-moths, which fly as strongly as small birds, also make northwards migrations. One of these is the death's head hawk-moth. In 1956 hundreds were recorded in Britain, a great swarm of them having evidently flown in from the south. The beautiful bedstraw hawk-moth is always a rarity. Years may go by without its being seen in northern Europe. Both these hawk-moths lay eggs in northern latitudes, and the caterpillars from them can be bred through to the adult stage with the aid of artificial heat. In the wild, however, they are all doomed to die during the winter.

Butterflies are welcome visitors everywhere, but the Mediterranean region also receives from North Africa occasional swarms of locusts, and sometimes these travel even farther north. In 1944, for example, a swarm appeared in the Gironde district of south-west France, and small bands of them in 1945. One swarm that flew over Bordeaux is said to have caused considerable excitement. In the following year an even larger invasion occurred and some swarms flew north, a few individuals reaching southern England. This happened again in 1947.

Bats occur throughout Europe, and it is a moot point where to include a brief note on the present status of bats. Since twenty-five of the total of twenty-eight European bats are found in some parts of the Mediterranean region—although not exclusively so—it seems right to discuss them here.

Reports of declining numbers of bats have come from all over Europe during the past few years. The decline is sufficiently serious to make fourteen governments, including that of the U.S.S.R., pass legislation to protect them. In some areas certain species have been extinguished and in others the populations are much reduced in numbers. The causes are manifold. They include the use of the insecticide D.D.T., to which bats are especially susceptible, and other poisons used as fumigants in churches and other buildings. In one house in Scotland, for example, 1,500 bats were killed in one day by fumigants. The objections to the presence of bats are the smell they make, the noise, the accumulation of guano, supposed damage to the fabric of the buildings—and superstition.

Some bats roost and hibernate in caves and tunnels of many kinds, a significant proportion of which have been used as rubbish tips or sealed for other reasons. Other bats use trees for both purposes, especially deciduous trees, sleeping in holes in the trunks or under bark. The widespread felling of broad-leaved trees, especially of old trees with loose bark, the planting of conifers instead of broad-leaved in re-afforestation schemes, the demolition of old buildings in favour of concrete blocks, as well as the accumulation of insecticides in their prey, have all had an impact. Not least, ironically enough, has been the increased interest shown by zoologists in the biology of bats, which has caused a marked decline through the deleterious effects of bat banding and disturbance in the hibernacula for study purposes, causing the bats to use up food reserves so that they do not survive the winter.

The new scientific interest in bats has revealed at least one unexpected benefit from these animals. Everyone has known for a long time that European bats all feed on insects. While it would be difficult to give a detailed analysis of the types of insects they eat and of the numbers, it is reasonable to say that they must eat huge quantities of them in the course of a year and that a high proportion of these must be inimical to man's interests. The unexpected benefit must be exemplified by a single observation, but the results of this can be multiplied many times. A single bat was seen in broad daylight to zigzag up the course of a stream at midday, not far from the surface of the water. Its passage was marked by hundreds of insects of all kinds that had fallen on the water and were vainly struggling to take wing again. The bat undoubtedly had caught many insects but had beaten down more to become food for fishes. Since any water surface at night has its quota of bats hawking over the surface, their onslaught on insects, plus the provision of fish food, must be a considerable benefit in aggregate.

Greater horseshoe bats sleeping in a cave. One of the most distinctive of the many species of bats inhabiting the Mediterranean area, it is named from the horseshoe-shaped folds of skin on the nose, used in echo-location. It wraps its wings around the body like a cloak when at rest.

The mountains

It has been said that there is hardly any mountain landscape in Europe which has not been modified by man. This may be exaggeration for the sake of effect. If true, it is largely because no European mountain reaches anything like the heights attained elsewhere in the world. The highest peak is in the French Alps, where Mont Blanc reaches 4,876 m., compared with Mount Everest at 8,848 m. Even so, these modest peaks still serve as climatic oases giving refuge to plants and animals not found in the surrounding lowlands. Such species have had to adapt to the peculiar conditions of high-altitude zones, notably a progressive lowering of the temperature and the increased amount of solar radiation. Small plants, for example, may have to tolerate, even at 2,100 m., a variation in temperature of 60°C between the upper parts, exposed to the direct rays of the sun, and the lower parts that are shaded.

For animals, increasing altitude means lowered temperatures and a reduction in atmospheric pressure with its concomitant, a reduced oxygen supply. This has meant physiological adaptation as well as the morphological adaptations to the physical nature of the ground. It also means adjustment to the local pattern of plant growth, from the lowermost or colline zone, through montane, sub-alpine and alpine zones to the snow zone at the tops of the highest mountains. This succession of zones corresponds closely to those at sea-level encountered from south to north, which begin with the deciduous forest and pass through the taiga, tundra and arctic zones. This means that we can expect to see forms that normally live in cold climates being found at high altitudes in the sub-tropics or even the tropics.

The mammal living at the highest altitude in Europe is the snow or alpine vole. This occurs in isolated populations in the Sierra Gredos of Spain, the Pyrenees, central Apennines, the Swiss Alps, the Balkans, Carpathians and the Tatra mountains of Czechoslovakia. In the Gard, of southern France, it occurs in the lowlands, but elsewhere it lives among loose rock and grass above the tree-line, even to the snow-line where there is suitable cover. It feeds on grasses and other herbs, including twigs of bilberry. It is 21 cm. total length, of which one-third is tail.

Insectivorous mammals are the scarcest of all in the mountains but the mole is found up to 1,300 m. and is important to the ecology because tree-seedlings develop far better on the old mounds that it has thrown up than elsewhere.

Better-known mammals of the alpine zone are the ibex and the marmot, and characteristic of the sub-alpine zone are the chamois and the mouflon. Of these four, none has had a greater impact than the first-named, the ibex or wild goat. To the non-specialist, the ibex and the goat are two distinct species. To the specialist, whether he is dealing with fossil or sub-fossil remains, with the history of the animals in relation to man's influence on them, or with the presently living animals, there is nothing but confusion. The one solid fact that emerges is that the goat was domesticated about 7,000 years ago, that it was responsible for the barrenness of the southern European mountain ranges from Spain to Greece, and that it was a major factor in the decline first of the Ancient Greek civilization and later of the Roman Empire.

Previous page: Ibex on a cliff face in the Gran Paradiso. The males live apart from the flocks of 20 to 30 females and young. They all rest at higher altitudes during the day, descending to feed at night on grass, heather, sedges and lichens.

The most celebrated member of Europe's abundant alpine flora, the edelweiss, grows on rocky ledges at high altitudes.

HAWKES/NHPA

Nehring's snow vole, 15 cm long excluding the 11 cm tail, is found only in a small area of Yugoslavia. Little is known of its habits. The same species is found as a sub-fossil in Hungary, suggesting that it had a much wider range in pre-historic Europe.

Right: An alpine meadow, rich with many varieties of flowers, against a background of snow-covered mountains.

Ibex resting on a rocky shelf with the valley far below. Its only enemy in former times was the wolf, which managed to prey upon it even in its mountain fastnesses.

The domestic goat (and the wild form from which it was derived) is named *Capra hircus*. What is believed to be the only wild stock on the island of Crete is named *C. aegagrus*. The Spanish ibex is *C. pyrenaica* and the ibex elsewhere is called *C. ibex*. Some zoologists have regarded all the isolated populations in southern Europe as representing each a different species; others have regarded them as sub-species of a single species. Interbreeding in zoos has resulted in fertile hybrids, which suggests they all belong to one species. The only way out of this dilemma is to follow Dr G. C. Corbet, in his *Terrestrial Mammals of Western Europe*, who maintains "it is useful at present" to consider that there are two species, the ibex *C. ibex* and the domestic goat *C. hircus*.

The ibex, with its large curved horns up to 1 m. long, is at present in the mountains of Spain and the Alps. In the sixteenth century it was widespread in the Alps but by the middle of the last century it was reduced to about 60 individuals in the Gran Paradiso range, just south of the Swiss-Italian frontier. In 1856, Victor Emmanuel II proclaimed the area in which they were living a royal hunting park, so that the ibex was protected, and this has been a national park since 1922.

By 1938 there were an estimated 3,000 ibexes in the park and they were spreading beyond its boundaries. During World War II many were killed by poachers and in 1945 only 419 were left. Under resumed protection their numbers rose again to nearly 3,000 and some were trapped and taken to Austria, Germany and the Carpathians, as well as to Switzerland, to the Swiss National Park in the Engadine, set aside in the mountains in 1914, as a special sanctuary for ibex.

In these areas the ibexes live in equilibrium with their environment, as would any wild goats. The damage done by the domestic goat is great because the animal has been kept in herds and is a browser, eating almost any form of vegetation down to the roots, even climbing trees to strip the foliage. In the days of sailing ships, goats were taken on long voyages to supply the crews with milk and meat. They were often put ashore on oceanic islands and in due course their ravages converted what had been earthly paradises covered with luxuriant vegetation into rocky deserts. Similar destruction has been caused on mainlands, and the deserts of Africa and Asia have been partly, sometimes wholly, the work of sheep and goat herding.

The sub-tropical countries of the Mediterranean were formerly covered with open canopy woods of

SIMON/COLEMAN

broad-leaved trees beneath which grew a rich undergrowth of shrubs and low evergreen trees. These forests clothed the land to an altitude of 1,200 m., and above this were woods of conifers. The trees were cut down, the ground was tilled in a prodigal agriculture, and herds of goats prevented regeneration. Rain and wind erosion did the rest. The mountain-sides and the lowlands became barren deserts. Greece, Italy and Spain still bear the marks, particularly in their mountains, of the denudation of the soil.

Goats in the wild live in balance with their habitat so long as there are predators to thin their ranks. Man not only destroyed the forests; he destroyed the animals living in them. The only other predators at high altitudes today are the large birds of prey, now that wolves, lynxes and bears have been so reduced in numbers. In the mountains of southern Europe these are the golden eagle and Bonelli's eagle.

The golden eagle enjoys a wide distribution in southern Europe, especially in the mountainous areas. It is widespread in the north also, in the Highlands of Scotland, the mountains of Scandinavia, across Finland and north Russia and the Baltic Provinces. A majestic bird with uniformly

FERNANDEZ/COLEMAN

Spanish imperial eagle at its nest, which is typically huge and conspicuous, built in a tall, isolated tree. There are two forms of this eagle, one in the Iberian peninsula, the other in eastern Europe, from northern Greece to southern Russia.

Left: Female golden eagle. Typically a bird of the mountains, but rare today compared with former numbers, golden eagles soar majestically. In level flight they can reach speeds of 100 mph.

dark plumage and a golden tinge on the head and nape, it glides and soars with only occasional wingbeats. Although typically a dweller on barren mountainsides, it sometimes has its eyries in mountain forests, on sea cliffs or in the lowlands. Its main prey is ptarmigan, red grouse, blue or mountain hare, and marmots, as well as the young of the mountain herbivores. The golden eagle may have a wingspan of nearly 2·5 m.

Bonelli's eagle, half the size of the golden eagle, but with powerful talons, is less well known, and is not so typically European. The largest numbers are found today in Spain, especially in the barren mountains of the central and southern parts of the country. It also occurs in the extreme south-east of France, in Corsica, Sardinia, Sicily, southern Italy and the southern Balkans. On the other side of the Mediterranean it is a familiar raptor of the Ethiopian highlands.

Both eagles normally kill on the ground, swooping down on their prey or skimming the ground to take it by surprise. Bonelli's eagle hunts rodents, hares and reptiles. It is also the chief enemy of the alpine chough. This is distinguished from the common chough by its yellow bill, instead of the red bill; it usually lives at higher altitudes than the common chough, feeding mainly on small invertebrates taken from rock crevices. It also eats some berries and other wild fruits. The mere appearance of Bonelli's eagle overhead is sufficient to panic the alpine choughs.

The golden eagle, especially, and Bonelli's eagle may take the occasional newborn ibex but the main hazards to young ibexes are gales, prolonged rains and snowstorms. Young and old are also in danger from falling rocks and avalanches. A count made in the Gran Paradiso Park in the winter of 1958–59 showed that 136 were killed by these last two hazards. A continuing danger, insidious rather than spectacular, to the ibex everywhere is the increase in grazing by domestic herds of goats and sheep and the steady expansion into the mountains of pasture and arable land.

The chamois is almost the symbol of the Alps and of the alpine zones of southern Europe. In western Europe it is still found in the Alps, the Pyrenees, the Cantabrian mountains and the Apennines. It also occurs in the Balkans, the Carpathians, the Tatra and the Sudeten. Its typical habitat is the alpine forest and round about the tree-line although it may go up to the snow-line in summer. On the whole, it lives at a lower altitude than the ibex. Chamois form small herds of females and young, led by an old female. The males are solitary, joining the herds during the rut only, between late October and December, single kids being born between April and June.

An important factor above a certain altitude is that food becomes progressively scarce. Above the last forest trees are the alpine meadows; higher still, scattered plants grow in rock crevices up to the snow-line or to the margins of glaciers. Such vegetation, covered for months in winter under snow and ice, offers a meagre source of food. Some mountain species go down into the forests at a lower level; a few hibernate.

Mountain mammals are relatively few in Europe. The varying hare is a glacial relic. In the lowland tundra it is known as the arctic hare. It is present in the Alps, on the Scandinavian and Scottish mountains, but not the Pyrenees, the Jura or the mountains of central Europe.

The most characteristic rodent of the European mountains is without doubt the marmot. It is plump-bodied, 50 cm. long, with the tail 19 cm., dark brown with brown-grey underparts. It is restricted to the Alps and the Carpathians, living on the alpine meadows especially on the sunny southern slopes. Diurnal, it lives in small colonies that probably correspond to families or groups of families, each family living in its separate burrow. The day is spent feeding on grasses and sunbathing near the entrance to the burrow. A shrill whistle from one of them, having sighted danger, sends the rest scuttling for safety. Towards the end of the summer, marmots lay in stores of hay in the burrow before going into hibernation about mid-October.

The mouflon, or wild sheep, probable ancestor of the domestic sheep, is indigenous to the mountains of Corsica and Sardinia, but has been introduced into Germany, France, Switzerland, Austria, Hungary and Italy. It is likely that the mouflon of the two Mediterranean islands are remnants forced into mountain refuges, and that the species originally ranged through lowland woodlands of

the Mediterranean region. Where it has been introduced it has become feral in lowland forests. The mouflon is gregarious, the rams living in separate flocks from the ewes and young.

Less conspicuous than the mammals but ecologically as important are the myriad invertebrates that live among the lichens and mosses and the small herbaceous plants growing in the cracks and crevices of seemingly barren rocky summits of mountains. These include spiders and mites and numerous small insects, many microscopic in size. It is a fauna exploited by one of the characteristic birds of the European mountains, the wall creeper.

Left: Chamois on a snowy, rocky slope. This is an inhabitant of the alpine zones of southern Europe, from the Cantabrian mountains to the Caucasus, grazing grasses, herbage and lichens and browsing the foliage of trees, including that of conifers.

The wild sheep of Europe, of which the mouflon shown here is one form, were originally probably as much animals of the steppes as of the mountains. Under persecution and domestication, only the wild remnants of the mountain forms were left. The mouflon proper is found today in Corsica and Sardinia.

This is the alpine counterpart of the tree creeper of lower altitudes, which searches the crevices in the bark of trees for anything edible, using its long curved bill to probe for them.

It is now established that birds have a keener eyesight than man, the best-sighted birds having about ten times the acuity of the human eye. This keener sight can be demonstrated at a simpler level by anyone who takes the trouble to look closely at the creviced bark of a tree. If this is followed by a closer scrutiny with a strong hand lens, it is something of a revelation to see how many small insects, spiders and other small invertebrates, as well as eggs and larvae, are sheltered in the bark. This is the rich, if scattered, food supply which the tree creeper exploits.

The wall creeper exploits a similar supply in rock crevices. About 16 cm. long, it is grey, crimson and black, and shows white spots on its rounded wings when in flight. It climbs vertical walls of rock, without help from its tail, probing the crevices with its long, slender, down-curved bill, for spiders, millipedes and the rest. The most fruitful faces of rock are those shaded from the sun, where the micro-habitats in the crevices are more humid than where there is prolonged exposure to the sun.

Wall creepers nest up to 2,500 m. and feed up to 5,000 m. in the Alps. Much of this habitat is shared with rock doves, crag martins, and alpine choughs, sometimes with rock nuthatches that have similar habits to the nuthatch of the lowlands.

As we have seen, the alpine chough's yellow bill distinguishes it from its close relative, the common chough. It is doubtful which of these two birds can claim to be the highest-living mountain bird. The common chough was the highest bird seen by an early expedition on Mount Everest where it breeds regularly up to 5,180 m., and at times at 5,700 m. It is, however, more numerous at lower altitudes, although apparently being ousted everywhere by the jackdaw. The even scarcer alpine chough tends to be confined more to the high mountains.

Moorlands and Marshes

Today, Europe, in common with other parts of the world, is facing a water famine. This is not surprising. The greater part of Europe has been slowly drying out since the warming of the climate caused what is usually referred to as the retreat of the ice-cap, at the end of the last Ice Age. Where the low-lying ground was well drained, the water from the melting glaciers soaked away, but in many places it has remained over larger or smaller areas to this day. The natural draining of the land has also been accelerated by man, who has drained the marshes in so many places, to give good agricultural land. He has also rid himself of one of the natural marsh-creating animals, the beaver. These are reasons why only a fraction remains of what would naturally be marsh.

To define what is meant by a marsh presents difficulties. There are certain areas which are sodden for most or all of the year. They may be wet with salt water or with fresh water and they are present in great variety. Depending on whether they are on elevated moorland or on lowland, near the sea or far inland, peaty and therefore acid, or alkaline, thoroughly waterlogged so that they form shallow lakes with protruding vegetation, or drying up for part of the year, they are called marshes, swamps, bogs, fens and other names besides. Here, the word "marsh" is used in the broadest sense.

Since the southern part of Europe, notably the Mediterranean region, was not covered in ice there are markedly fewer marshes there than in the north. Those that do exist are mainly in the deltas of large rivers. Examples are the *Marismas* near the delta of the Guadalquivir in Spain, the Camargue, in the valley of the Rhône, three areas along the Adriatic coast of Italy, and the delta of the Danube in Rumania. The last-named can only barely be included in the Mediterranean region but faunistically it belongs to it. There is another large delta to the east, that of the Volga. Also in the Mediterranean region are large areas of marsh that have been drained. One is the valley of the Po, the other is the famous Pontine marshes which defied all efforts to drain them until the present century.

Large areas of marsh in the northern part of Europe have disappeared, notably on the north German plain. In the Netherlands, and to a lesser extent in eastern England, much marshland has been reclaimed. There remains a great deal of marshland in Finland and the northern half of Russia, including the vast Pripet marshes.

How prevalent marshland was in the past is indicated by two archaeological features. The first is the so-called lake dwellings, or pile dwellings, the most famous being those unearthed in Switzerland. It was probably common for prehistoric man to build his huts on stilts on marshland or at the edges of lands. The usual theory is that he did so for security from wild beasts. In other places the sites of prehistoric villages are hills, partly because the valleys were both forested and marshy. In many places the valleys were still swampy within the memory of people still living, although drainage has made them dry now.

Swamps, then, are havens for persecuted animals. In the *Marismas*, for example, the wild boar and red deer find sanctuary. But swamps also have their problems for people living in them, and in some of these areas the people used to go about on stilts. In others they had their boats ready for winter flooding. The birds that use swamps are especially swimming birds, such as ducks and geese, and the waders, the birds that have long legs and long beaks for probing the muddy ground.

Because marshes, so long as they are not drained, remain undisturbed, their faunas have remained stable and relatively unaltered. Much of their animal life consists of microscopic creatures, many swarming near the surface. Invisible to the naked eye, or nearly so, they not only play a vital role in maintaining the natural equilibrium but are part of a food chain supporting the larger animals. This is brought out when we consider the group of birds that are more characteristic than any other of marshy places. These are the so-called waders, of the family Scolopacidae (order Charadriiformes) and related species, such as plovers.

The common chough on an estuarine shore, its glossy blue-black plumage and curved, red bill and red legs unmistakable. Its normal home is cliffs and rocky outcrops near the sea but it ranges also into the mountains to join the alpine chough.

Cattle on the Camargue, the delta of the Rhone, where two branches of the river enclose a subtropical area of water and mud famous for its rich fauna, especially for its flamingoes.

In many parts of the world the domesticated horse has gone feral, that is, it has returned to the wild and breeds without human intervention. One of the more famous breeds of feral horses in Europe is the Exmoor pony of south-west England, seen here.

Waders are dumpy, medium-sized birds seen especially in winter on estuarine or other mudflats, usually standing well spaced out, sometimes 1,000 at a time. They tend to find their way to coastal flats or coastal marshes in winter but in summer are distributed over a variety of habitats and nesting places.

The typical wader has fairly strong legs and a moderately long bill, of the shape associated with probing the ground for worms and insects. The snipe breeds all over Europe north of the Mediterranean region. It is easily distinguished from all other waders by its dark plumage with light stripes. Most waders are a cryptically mottled brown or grey, lighter on the underparts. The snipe is 20 cm. long with a straight 6 cm.-long bill; it lives in wet habitats of all kinds, from valleys to elevated moorlands, where it probes the soft ground with its sensitive bill for worms, or picks up insects, snails, slugs and seeds on the ground. It nests in coarse grass or rushes. The very similar but rather smaller jack snipe, which lives in a similar habitat to the snipe, eats more seeds. It nests in wet swamps in north-eastern Europe but moves to western and south-western Europe for the winter.

The related black-tailed godwit, 40 cm. long, nests in a scrape in the grass on boggy moors. It wades as deep into water as its 20 cm.-long legs permit, and probes the mud with its long, straight beak. Contrasting with this the common sandpiper

A marsh bird with its stronghold mainly in the Danube valley is the little egret. Snow-white, with a black bill, black legs and yellow feet, it nests in colonies, often in company with other herons.

The spoonbill, national bird of the Netherlands, breeds elsewhere mainly in the valley of the Danube. Its habitat is marshes and mud-flats, now made rare in Europe as land is drained for agricultural and industrial use. The spoonbill has been grievously persecuted by man.

Left: The flamingo's odd-shaped bill is adapted for filtering minute planktonic food from the water. Its pink colour is due to a carotenoid pigment obtained from the algae on which it feeds.

One bird that has suffered little from the change from virgin land to cultivated soil is the lapwing plover. Its natural home is moors, marshes and mud-flats, but. it is as commonly seen in flocks on arable land. It lays its eggs in a shallow depression in the ground.

ROBERTS/ARDEA

LANGSBURY/COLEMAN

A snipe sits tight on her nest. This is a secretive marsh bird, well concealed by its mottled brown plumage, difficult to observe until flushed. Then it can be recognized by its long straight bill and its characteristic zig-zag flight.

Above, right: Except for a few small areas, the common sandpiper breeds all over Europe beside any kind of water, rivers, lakes, hill-streams, even sewage farms. Its shrill voice, constant bobbing of head and tail when settled and its flight low over water distinguish it from other small waders.

FOGDEN/COLEMAN

One way to travel over marshes is with stilts, which is precisely what one bird, the black-winged stilt, does. In its case the stilts are its own absurdly long pink legs. Its main areas of distribution are at the western and eastern extremes of southern Europe.

Avocet with nest of four eggs at the water's edge. A close relative of the black-winged stilt, with similar long legs, but with more white in the plumage and an upturned long, slender bill, it is mainly found in southern Europe but also occurs along the coastal mud-flats of the Netherlands to the German Baltic.

BROEKHUYSEN/ARDEA

Far right: The epitome of statuesque patience is the grey heron, a river- or lake-side bird common all over Europe, except in the north and south-west. Its habit is to stand motionless for long periods of time in or near water waiting to snap up fish, frog, vole or small bird with its long, dagger-like bill.

runs along the water's edge of lakes and streams. It has the same build as a snipe but uses its straight bill to pick insects off stones, sometimes wading to get them. The dunlin seeks worms and other small invertebrates, tapping and probing the mud for them. Entirely different tactics are used by the phalaropes, belonging to the related family Phalaropidae. They look like waders but they swim pivoting on the surface of the water, stirring up the mud, so bringing small animals to the surface.

Recalling more completely the habits of certain marsh-dwelling humans is the black-winged stilt, a typical marsh-dwelling bird. It measures 38 cm., has handsome white underparts and black wings, with a bill 6 cm. long used for picking food off the surface as it wades on its slender pink legs which are 25 cm. in length. The avocet looks not unlike a stilt, its white body with black markings perched on absurdly long slender legs. Its long bill, delicately up-curved, is swept from side to side to skim small animals from the surface.

Larger birds with stilt-like legs are the herons, the most widespread of which in Europe is the grey heron, standing nearly 1 m. high. It breeds over most of Europe except in the south-west and the north, but being a partial migrant it can be seen outside the breeding season in all but northern Scandinavia and Finland. It spends long periods of time motionless beside a pool or stream. Otherwise it walks slowly and cautiously looking for frogs, fish, water voles, young birds, molluscs, crustaceans and insects. It nests in tall trees, often well away from water, the nests being added to year by year to form large saucers of sticks. Herons nest in colonies, with numerous nests in a clump of tall trees, the whole being called a heronry. Their fidelity to the nesting site, although it may be deserted for most of the year, is such that some heronries are reputed to be 1,000 years old.

The habits of the grey heron emphasize the difficulty of drawing a hard-and-fast line, at least ecologically, between the areas of marshy or swampy grounds and lakes or even streams and rivers. As to the latter, a marsh usually has at least a rivulet or a stream running through it, or a lake adjacent to it. In all such places a heron can satisfy its food requirements. So the grey heron may be found feeding in marshes, shallow lakes, rivers, streams, even sheltered tidal waters. As well as nesting in trees, the grey heron may nest in bushes, reed-beds, on the ground or on cliffs.

The purple heron and the night heron, mainly found in the Mediterranean region, are more given

to marshes, the former nesting in reed-beds, the latter in these also but more often in trees. The great white heron is an inhabitant of the Danube basin, as is the little egret. The bittern, another member of the heron family, also frequents a variety of wet habitats, except in northern Europe. Its fame rests partly on the booming call of the male in the breeding season and partly on its camouflage. It is a long-necked, short-legged heron, its brown plumage streaked and patterned with black. Much play is made of the way a bittern in a reed bed stretches its neck vertically so that the black streaks running down the neck give it invisibility against a background of reeds. In fact, its plumage is such that a bittern against any background, in any position and from any angle, is hard to detect, the incredible camouflage effect of its plumage needing to be experienced at first-hand to be believed.

If a bird had to be chosen to represent the spirit of the moors and marshes and the mud-flats it would be the curlew. It is one of the largest of the waders, a bird with a long down-curved bill. Its repeated calls, *coor-lee*, have an air of wistful loneliness appropriate to the wildness of its habitat.

While the curlew may represent the spirit of the marsh, there are two contenders for the role of representing the abundance of the marsh. The first is the ducks, the second the two-winged flies.

Ducks typical of marshes include the teal, garganey, gadwall, wigeon, pintail and shoveler, and on the marshes or the wet meadows there are geese. All are numerous enough in the more inaccessible and the large marshes, but everywhere their numbers are nothing like as great as formerly. This is particularly true of the more heavily populated areas of western Europe where, if the accounts in old books are to be believed, ducks lived in indescribable numbers on the marshes, until they were heavily shot up.

Today, numbers are more associated with the two-winged flies, the mosquitoes and midges, and especially the non-biting midges, or chironomids. These are soft-bodied, almost colourless, two-winged insects bearing a slight resemblance to gnats. The males have bushy antennae and large eyes. The larvae are red and are known as blood-worms. Their blood contains haemoglobin, enabling them to live in waters of low oxygen content,

BURTON/COLEMAN

The pintail of northern Europe is a slender, long-necked duck with a thin, pointed tail. A shy bird that quickly takes flight if disturbed, it feeds on aquatic plants or, on the coasts, on eelgrass.

Left: The common bittern lives in dense reed beds of marshes, backwaters and lakes. A relative of the herons, it is remarkable for the camouflage effect of its brown, mottled and barred plumage.

Far left: The purple heron of southern Europe, with a smaller population in the Netherlands and northern France, is smaller than the grey heron. It frequents reed beds and bushes near lakes and rivers, its long toes enabling it to walk over soft ground and floating weeds.

feeding on bacteria, small fungi, algae and protozoans.

The larvae pupate early in the day; the adults emerge in late afternoon and then, in their thousands, form dancing swarms that rise and fall in relation to a fixed point. This may be a post or a tree and, with a tree especially, the swarm may appear like a cloud of smoke rising from it. Nearer the ground the swarm, which consists of males indulging in their nuptial flight, 18,000 of them weighing only a gramme, may form a curtain 100 metres long and 2 metres high, like a curtain of mist. The females join the swarm singly to mate, then depart to lay their eggs in stagnant water.

These dancing swarms on summer evenings are regarded as a sign of good weather on the next day, which is largely true. The swarming is much affected by wind, air-currents and rain. Even a light breeze is enough to make them settle and wait for fine weather.

This recalls a question commonly asked: how far can the behaviour of animals be taken as a forecast of weather to come? It has been established in recent years that swifts will fly off in a stream at right angles to the path of an oncoming electric storm, returning when the storm has passed. There are other examples of the kind, and there is a fish in central and eastern Europe, a loach, that is known as the weatherfish. It is an elongate, almost cylindrical, grey-brown fish up to 35 cm. long and lives in lakes and river backwaters, especially in stagnant waters. Where there is a deficiency in oxygen, the loach can come to the surface, gulp air and use its intestine as a lung. During the day it buries itself in the mud or sand and becomes active at night, but it is said to be extremely sensitive to changes in barometric pressure, becoming increasingly active at the approach of storms.

Large lakes do more than provide a habitat for aquatic plants and animals. They serve as a reserve of water to the countryside around.

Life in Freshwater: Lakes

The name "limnology" was given to the study of lakes by the Swiss biologist F. A. Forel towards the end of the nineteenth century. It has since been used to include the study of all freshwaters. *Limné*, in its original Greek, seems to have been used for a marsh, a lake or a marshy lake. This is most appropriate since puddle, pond, marsh and lake are steps in a sequence, with all gradations between. A lake, as usually understood, is a large body of standing water sufficiently deep in the middle to prevent anchored plants from reaching the surface. It is not still water in an absolute sense because there will be convection currents, currents caused by wind action on the surface as well as movement wherever a spring, stream or river enters a lake. It is, however, relatively still, which gives us the difference between a lake and a river. The stillness has an important bearing on the life of the inhabitants.

Some lakes have been formed by glacial action, others have arisen through the rocks under the soil having been dissolved away, with a subsequent sinking of the surface. Yet others have been formed by volcanic action or where a landslide has blocked the entrance to a valley—or where man has built a dam to create a reservoir lake. Some lakes have gently sloping shores covered with abundant vegetation. In others the edges of the lake rise steeply and little vegetation is visible in them. In all, the animal life is dependent on vegetation, either in the form of plants or, and more importantly, in the form of plant plankton.

The plant life, whether macroscopic plants or microscopic plankton, is food for the "converters", those animals, microscopic to large, that feed exclusively on it. The converters in turn are eaten by the predators. The food chain is, therefore, no different from that on land, although sometimes more complex.

The converters are for the most part crustaceans, worms, molluscs and insect larvae. The predators are mainly insect larvae and fishes, certain water birds and otters, although the last of these is more typical of rivers.

The main converters are the very small crustaceans, including *Daphnia,* the water flea. There are a number of species, the largest, *D. magna,* being 5 mm. long. Apart from the head, with two pairs of prominent antennae, the rest of the body and limbs is enclosed in a rounded carapace of chitin. This carapace is transparent, and under the microscope the internal organs and the beating of the heart

can be seen. So also can the eggs, carried in a brood pouch between the body and the back of the carapace, for all *Daphnia* are female, reproducing parthenogenetically (the so-called virgin birth). Under certain circumstances, at the approach of winter or during prolonged drought, some of the eggs hatch to males. The eggs they fertilize are resistant to adverse conditions, and are called "winter eggs".

At times *Daphnia* are so numerous they form reddish or brownish patches in the water, red because when oxygen is scarce, as in overcrowding, the haemoglobin in the blood increases. At all times, this crustacean swims with jerks of its antennae. At each jerk the animal jumps upwards in the water, then pauses and sinks slowly down, and follows this with another upward jerk, giving the appearance of a flea jumping.

Another familiar crustacean is *Cyclops*, 2–3 mm. long, pear-shaped with broad end in front, and with the long pair of antennae used in swimming, although the legs on the underside of the thorax are the main swimming organs. Behind is a forked "tail" at the base of which the females carry a pair of prominent egg-sacs. The scientific name for this crustacean refers to its single large eye in the centre of the head. Like *Daphnia*, *Cyclops* feeds on minute algae and bacteria.

Another familiar freshwater crustacean is the light-brown shrimp *Gammarus*. This is not a true shrimp, which is marine. The males are 18 mm. long, the females slightly smaller. *Gammarus* is flattened from side to side and it swims on its side, propelling itself with its strong thoracic legs and the last three pairs of smaller abdominal legs. It lives under stones or skids along over the surface of mud. Its gills are at the bases of the first four pairs of thoracic legs.

Snails and slugs on land may be a nuisance to the gardener but they are primarily composters and scavengers, feeding mainly on dead or dying vegetation and thinning out seedlings. The same role is performed by the pond snails. How numerous these are can be seen when a pond dries out during a drought. As its margin recedes so the snails migrate towards the centre until finally there is a carpet of shells. The three main kinds are the pond snails with conical, spiral shells; ramshorn snails with a shell coiled like a ram's horn; and the bladder snails in which the front part of the shell is enlarged and bladder-like. All rasp away at vegetation, living or dead, with the ribbon-like

Left: Man's growing need of an adequate water supply has led to the harnessing of natural lakes and the creation of artificial ones, as reservoirs, like this one at Arlington in south-west England. While benefiting man, reservoirs also provide new habitats for aquatic animals and water birds.

Cyclops, a freshwater copepod crustacean of minute size, named after the one-eyed giant of Greek mythology, is a common constituent of the freshwater plankton. It carries its eggs in a pair of oval sacs at the base of the tail.

Pond snail eating the dead larva of a water beetle. Although pond snails eat almost anything, vegetable or animal, they take mainly animal food.

119

GOODERS/ARDEA

NEWMAN/NHPA

tongue beset with rows of horny teeth. The limpets do likewise. They have conical shells, with the apex slightly tilted, and cling firmly to stones or water plants.

Bivalve molluscs are represented by freshwater mussels and cockles, both of which lie two-thirds buried in the mud. To feed, they gape and draw water in through a siphon. The water passes across their lattice-work gills, which extract from it oxygen and minute particles of organic matter for food, passing this to the stomach. They are agents in keeping water clean.

Anyone who has indulged in the sport of pond-hunting knows the great variety of animals that can be caught in a gauze net. When the contents of the net are emptied into a dish of water they convey some idea of the infinite variety of active life in fresh water. The result will be much the same whether the net has been drawn through a village pond or through Lake Lagoda, near Leningrad. One of the more prominent items in the catch will be the caddis-worms, larvae of a flying insect with two pairs of gauzy wings. Caddis-worms live in tubes of their own construction, made of pieces of leaf, sticks, tiny pebbles or small molluscs' shells, bound together with silk. The larva pushes its front part out of the tube to crawl along on its three pairs of legs, to eat plant or even animal food.

Caddis-worms need a protective case if only to counter the rapacity of dragonfly larvae. In contrast to the adults, dragonfly larvae are dull and mud-coloured, but like them they are carnivorous. There are two kinds, the adults of which are known respectively as dragonflies and damselflies. The former, when resting, hold their two pairs of long gauzy wings sideways. Damselflies are smaller and hold their wings over their backs. Both hunt other insects, seizing them in flight. The larvae use what

is called a mask when feeding. The rear pair of the mouthparts are fused and jointed and can be shot out and withdrawn to lie folded under the face, like a mask. At the end are two claws. The mask is shot out at prey, which is caught by the claws and brought back to the mouth to be eaten. Prey is any animal that can be overpowered, from small insect larvae to small fishes.

Size is not always an indication of evil intent in insects. One of the largest European water beetles is the great silver beetle, so called from the silvery reservoirs of air carried on its underside. It is 45 mm. long, dark brown with short antennae. The beetle uses elongated mouthparts as feelers. To breathe, it rises to the surface, breaks the surface film with its antennae, and draws air under its wing-cases and into the two reservoirs on its underside. It feeds on water plants, so lives among waterside vegetation. The female great silver beetle lays her fifty eggs in a silken bag and attaches this to water plants. The larvae feed on water snails.

The great diving beetle is carnivorous as an adult as well as a larva. It is 30 mm. long and in rising to the surface to take in air it pushes the tip of the abdomen through the surface film. The great diving beetle will kill anything up to a moderate-

The magnificent emperor dragonfly, blue-bodied in the male, green in the female, resting on a reed. Dragonflies are the hawks of the insect world, feeding on other insects caught on the wing. Each male patrols a fixed territory along a river, driving other males away.

The large red damselfly laying her eggs. Damselflies are small dragonflies that differ from the dragonflies proper most obviously in their habit of folding the wings over the back when at rest instead of spreading them.

sized frog, and its larva is almost equally voracious.

The water scorpion is flattened and leaf-shaped, a dark brown bug up to 30 mm. long with a tail, but the tail has no sting. It is a straight tube, to be pushed through the surface film to take in air. The two front legs are large and folded like a jack-knife and are used for grasping prey into which the water scorpion plunges its beak to suck the body juices. One species is elongated, up to 60 mm. long with a narrow body, and is sometimes called a water stick insect.

The water boatman is also a bug, up to 18 mm. long and brownish; it rows itself through the water with oar-like hind legs. Water boatmen swim near the bottom and feed on small organic particles, but must periodically rise to the surface to take in air. Near relatives are the backswimmers, similar in build and habits but swimming on the back, which is keeled, making the insect even more boat-like. Backswimmers are predatory, seizing tadpoles or small fishes and sucking the life out of them with a piercing beak.

Two kinds of bugs use the surface film, the water measurers or water gnats and the pond skaters. The first has a long slender body with long legs spread sideways. It feeds on small insects that fall

BURTON/COLEMAN

BURTON/COLEMAN

The water spider of Europe is unique in being the only spider living wholly in water. It spins a diving bell of silk, like an inverted thimble anchored to water plants and fills this with bubbles of air brought from the surface trapped in the bristles on its body.

Above, left: Male of the great diving beetle, a highly carnivorous aquatic insect. The larva is also carnivorous, and both have strong sickle-shaped jaws to catch worms, water snails, other insects, tadpoles and fish.

on to the surface, as do the pond skaters, similar but larger insects, that also glide over the surface, their weight insufficient to break the surface film of the water.

Whirligig beetles, tiny oval beetles that gyrate on the surface of still waters, have the best of both worlds. Like the water boatman, a whirligig beetle can fly, and often does so, parachuting down once it is over a suitable stretch of water, also using its open wing-cases as a brake on its descent. Once it hits the water and closes its wings it is transformed into a submarine, carrying an air bubble with it. Its habit is, however, to swim at the surface, its eyes in two parts, one for seeing above water, the other to see under water.

The adaptations for breathing, by gills or by taking in air, found in many water insects, are outstripped by those of the water spider. It lives under water but needs air, so it spins an inverted bell of silk among water plants. Then it goes to the surface, traps a bubble of air in the bristles

Below, left: One of the most familiar insects on still or slow-flowing fresh waters is the small, black whirligig beetle. Groups of these beetles can be seen, especially in summer, gyrating on the surface at random. They never collide, being warned of each other's presence by the ripples they send out.

The natural range of the goldfish is from eastern Europe to China, but as a result of introduction it is now widespread in the fresh waters of Europe.

TWEEDIE/NHPA

HEATHER ANGEL

Male stickleback at its nest. The three-spined stickleback can live equally in fresh, brackish or salt water throughout the northern hemisphere. No freshwater fish has been more fully studied for its courtship behaviour and breeding habits. Here, the male, with its red throat, is indicating by nodding movements where the entrance to the nest is, while the female (above) watches.

Below, right: Young pike live in the weedy shallows of streams, rivers and lakes, usually just off the bottom. At first they feed on small animals like cyclops, later taking larger invertebrates. By the time they are about 20 cm. long their food is almost all fish.

The common perch is readily identifiable by its greenish brown body, red or orange lower fins and the dark bars across the back. A good food fish when well grown, it is little used although it takes a bait readily and is widely distributed.

covering its body, and dives with this to the bell, releasing it inside. It continues these trips until the bell is full of air.

Prehistoric man may have been aware of some of the larger insects of the fresh waters even if he was not especially interested in them. He would, however, have been interested in the fish, particularly when he built his dwellings over lakes. That interest continued in his descendants down to the present day. Indeed, man's interest in freshwater fishing has been responsible for many changes in the locations of the fishes themselves, more perhaps in rivers, but to some extent also in the lakes. Some species have been transported from one lake to another. Species from other countries have been introduced, for example, goldfish and the horned pout, and an American catfish which is now widespread in Europe.

There are only a score or so of fishes in European lakes, far fewer than there are in the rivers. Nearly half of these are also found in rivers. One of the most widespread as well as the most abundant of Europe's fishes is the well-known three-spined stickleback. It is found also in northern Asia and North America, and it is present in all fresh waters except fast-flowing hill streams or in mountain areas.

The three-spined stickleback is famous for its courting behaviour. The male builds a nest of plant material stuck together with secretions from his kidneys, in a shallow depression, usually on a sandy bottom. He then patrols an area around the nest, displaying his red chest and waiting for a female heavy with eggs to swim by. He dances before her, enticing her to the nest and nudges her in to lay her eggs. When she leaves by the other side he enters and sheds his milt on the eggs to fertilize them. Thereafter he guards the eggs and later the young. The young fish feed on midge

123

larvae, *Daphnia* and *Cyclops*. Older fish feed on worms, molluscs, freshwater shrimps and the larger insect larvae.

The bitterling also has interesting breeding habits. The female of this fish grows a long ovipositor and uses this to lay her eggs in the gills of a freshwater mussel. The male sheds his milt to fertilize them. While this is going on, the mussel releases its larvae, which cling to the bitterling's gill covers, to be carried around until ready to settle down and change into bivalves.

The charr, related to salmon and trout, have a wide range in the northern latitudes, in rivers, lakes and the sea. They are characteristic of deep lakes, and where they have been studied, as in Lake Windermere in north-west England, and in Lac Leman, Geneva, they spawn at depths of 20–100 m., from November to March at temperatures of 4–6° C. Charr feed on planktonic crustaceans, including *Daphnia*, insect larvae, freshwater shrimps, molluscs and fish.

The diet of the well-known perch is similar. This is a fish that as an adult lies close to or among solid objects such as the piles of a landing stage or bridge, tree roots, reeds or large stones. It readily takes a bait but only larger individuals are eaten.

A large catfish, the wels, up to 5 m. long in the eastern parts of its range, olive green with paler underparts, forms the basis of a valuable fishery in Russia and elsewhere in eastern Europe. It has a palatable flesh and its skin can be made into a leather. During May to July the females lay heaps of eggs on a mound of leaf litter where they are guarded by the male. The eggs are sometimes used to adulterate caviar. The wels has been successfully introduced into central England, but most attempts to introduce it into other parts of Europe have failed. It feeds on fishes, frogs, birds and small mammals.

Although so dissimilar in appearance, the wels and the pike have much in common, in their range of habitat and food. The wels lives in the still waters of lakes, lagoons and marshes, in backwaters of rivers and in the deep reaches of large rivers. The pike, widespread across Europe except in the Mediterranean region and Norway, lives among weeds in lakes, rivers and streams. It feeds mainly on fishes, of almost any kind including young pike, and it will also take frogs, newts and occasionally water birds and mammals, so its diet is much the same as the wels.

Certain animals seem destined to act as a food

Common European toad (left) and the natterjack or running toad. The latter lives where the soil is sandy, up to over 1,000 metres. Its short legs prevent it from leaping but it can run fast.

Above, left: The alpine newt lives in the mountains of southern Europe, up to 3,000 metres or more. It enters the water to breed from February to May. Sometimes it will stay all winter in water. At high altitudes the summer may be too short for the larvae to develop in one season.

The European or fire salamander, of the damp woods of west, central and southern Europe, is famous for the long-standing belief that it can pass unharmed through fire. The female visits a stream to deliver her gilled larvae, born alive.

reserve for a major part of the animal kingdom. Earthworms are an example. They function to keep the soil sweet, by aerating it and turning it, as well as composting it by dragging dead leaves into their burrows. Yet these universal gardeners form the prey of amphibians, reptiles, birds and mammals, to such a degree that it seems a miracle their numbers have not long ago declined. The same can be said of the amphibians, but with them their high rate of reproduction more obviously offsets the high mortality, both on land and in water where they breed. Although most of them spend so much of their active life on land, their usual breeding places are still waters, from marshes to ponds and lakes. This is therefore an appropriate place to make a brief review of the amphibians of Europe.

Amphibians are of two kinds, the tailed amphibians including newts and salamanders, and the tailless amphibians, the frogs and toads. There are thirty-nine species in Europe, eighteen being tailed amphibians. The most widespread of the newts is the great crested or warty newt, up to 17 cm. long, ranging from the British Isles to central Russia, and from the Alps to 60°N. The smaller smooth newt is mainly in central and northern

Europe, the palmate newt in western Europe. The alpine newt is typically in the mountains of the northern Mediterranean region, but extends north to the Netherlands and northern Germany, and eastwards to Russia. The marbled newt is mainly Mediterranean, the Iberian newt is confined to Iberia, and the Carpathian newt to the Carpathians, Tatra and Black Mountains.

The nine salamanders include the spotted or fire salamander, reputed by legend to be able to live in fire. The legend seems to have arisen by distortion from Aristotle's comment to his students, to the effect that its skin is so cold one would almost expect it to be able to pass through fire unharmed. Two of the others are the alpine salamander, of the Juras and Albania, which lives at between 800 to 3,000 m., and the olm, the long, pink, blind salamander of the caves of Dalmatia, which lives permanently in water and retains its gills throughout life. Most of the twenty-one tailless amphibians are found in southern Europe. A few are found throughout Europe.

The common toad is widespread north of the Alps; the natterjack or running toad ranges from western Europe to Poland. Toads have a strong homing instinct and an individual will rest daily in the same spot for years, returning to it after foraging. The common toad also migrates, in a direct line to its breeding pond, and it is now fairly certain it uses celestial navigation.

The green frog is found in southern, western and central Europe, and it also ranges into Asia and North Africa. The spadefoot toad, with a horny "spade" on the outer edge of the foot, for digging backwards into sandy soil, ranges from France to the Balkans and from Sweden to the Alps. In western Europe is the yellow-bellied toad, and in eastern Europe the fire-bellied. Both carry more poison than is usual in toads and, when danger threatens, they expose the yellow or red patches on their underside, as a warning that they have unpleasant qualities. The midwife toad, the male of which acts as nursemaid, lives in western Europe. He pushes his hind legs through the strings of eggs as the female lays them, and thereafter takes care of them, going to water periodically to immerse the eggs, and he finally takes them to water when they are about to hatch.

The grass frog, often called the common frog,

The edible frog has the doubtful honour of having its hindlegs coveted by human gastronomes. It lives in ponds, ditches and backwaters, quickly jumping into water and burying itself in mud when disturbed.

As the female midwife toad lays her string of eggs the male passes his hindlegs through the skein. Thereafter he is responsible for caring for them, finally taking them to water when they are about to hatch.

The European or green tree frog, of central and southern regions, is the only representative of its kind in Europe. It has the usual adhesive discs on all its toes for clinging to vertical surfaces. It breeds in water and moves in mid-summer to bushes and trees.

ranges from west to east and from the Alps to 70°N. The similar marsh and edible frogs range approximately from Holland to the Urals, the moor frog having a similar range but not extending so far west. The agile frog and the spotted mud or parsley frog are more localized, the first in Dalmatia, the second in northern Italy, France and Spain. Finally, there is the tree frog, in western and central Europe.

Amphibians generally make use of small ponds but will use the margins of large stretches of water, even slow flowing streams or canals, similar habitats to the moorhen or water hen. The moorhen's near relative, the coot, frequents the larger lakes, often in company with ducks, especially the mallard, *the* wild duck, that is present all over Europe on any kind of water.

BEAMES/ARDEA

BURTON/COLEMAN

Above: The mallard is the ancestor of the domesticated or farm-yard duck, and is the common wild duck of the northern hemisphere. It is found all over Europe, except in the extreme north of Scandinavia. Mallards spend much of their time on land, and feed on berries, seeds, leaves and insects as well as on water animals.

Large areas of water are preferred by the coot, a dumpy, slate-black water bird with a white frontal shield and beak. Coots have their own aerial barrage against winged predators. Several together sit on their tails and splash water into the air with their feet.

Little grebe, or dabchick, on its nest. It has the remarkable tactic against enemies of diving quickly at the first disturbance or sign of danger and remaining submerged, to reappear some distance from the spot where it dived.

ENGLAND/ARDEA

The delta of the Guadalquivir, in Spain, is not only the end of a river, but also forms part of one of Europe's largest remaining marshes.

Life in Freshwater: Rivers

A river differs from a lake in one fundamental respect: the water is moving, and in one direction except when tidal. A river is also colder than a lake, and contains more oxygen. These are points to remember when removing fishes from a river, and especially a shallow, fast-flowing river, to an aquarium. There are many more types of environment in a river, as can be seen by following a hypothetical river from its source to the sea.

The source of a river may be in a limestone cave, from a lake or from the lower end of a glacier. Usually it is on high ground, and starts as a spring or a mountain tarn, perhaps no more than a few small trickles of water that must unite before it is possible to see that this is the origin. Even then the water will be shallow, with algae, mosses and liverworts the only vegetation, and the only animals will be those feeding on the minute particles they filter from the water, such as rotifers or wheel animalcules and insect larvae. Small water snails will scrape algae from the stones.

When the headstreams have united, the greater volume of water cuts a course through the ground and the flow is more rapid. The steeper the slope the faster the flow, and the water washes the stones of the bed clean as the stream becomes a torrent. The only animals able to live here are those that can cling to or shelter under the stones to avoid being swept away, such as the larvae of stoneflies and of certain mayflies.

Soon the river reaches more level ground, at lower altitudes, and its pace slackens. Instead of a bed of clean-washed pebbles, particles of soil and of organic debris, hitherto held in suspension, drop to the bottom, especially at a bend in the river. As more and more of this is deposited, mud accumulates in which plants take root, particularly near the margins of the river, and more and more plants can grow. Aquatic worms and freshwater mussels live in the mud. Among the stems of the water plants are found the larvae of water beetles, caddis-worms and the burrowing larvae of mayflies.

Rivers vary greatly from swift-flowing to sluggish, from narrow to broad, from limpid to discoloured with a load of alluvium in suspension, from shallow to deep. Usually, the upper reaches are swift, the middle reaches flowing less swiftly and the lower reaches often meandering, winding in broad loops, and sometimes emptying into the sea by many mouths where the deposited alluvium has formed a delta. There may be stagnant backwaters, bays of still water or bordering marshes. So is provided a wide variety of habitats.

Salmon spend most of their lives in the sea, feeding and growing, often several hundred miles from the mouth of the stream where they were hatched. At the end of this time they return to their natal stream, surmounting obstacles such as waterfalls to reach it.

The dace prefers clear, moderately fast-running streams and rivers, but may also be found in lakes. It occurs over much of Europe and though often fished, it has little value as food. The fish shown here does not display the typical colours.

A scene reminiscent of Canada today, but once familiar all over Europe: a beaver eating bark, with the beaver pond, its containing dam and the beaver lodge (the animal's home) at the centre of the pond. The European beaver is now only found in small numbers in Scandinavia, European Russia, and in the valleys of the Elbe and the Rhône. Under natural conditions beaver ponds served as reservoirs of water, irrigating the countryside.

As if handed down from our prehistoric ancestors, who first saw the river as a source of food, the animals most associated in our minds with rivers are its fishes. These therefore must take pride of place here, and of Europe's more than fifty kinds of fishes it is convenient to start with those which, by their adaptability, can be found in almost any type of water. The three-spined stickleback has already been mentioned. This 7–10 cm. fish is probably the most familiar, widespread and abundant of Europe's fishes. It lives in all waters except swift mountain or hill streams, even in estuarine or coastal waters, and is sometimes found well out to sea. A well-studied fish, it is perhaps best known for the male's care of eggs and young.

The more slim-bodied, slightly larger minnow is also abundant in most streams and lakes, some-

times in ponds, thriving best in clear-flowing water with a gravel bed. The minnow is found up to 1,981 m. in the Alps.

The deep-bodied, bluish-green roach, with reddish ventral fins, 15–20 cm. long, with a maximum of 35 cm., is also common and widespread in all kinds of water, from small ponds and rivers up to 914 m. altitude. It lives on plants and animal foods, the latter comprising a wide range of invertebrates. In eastern Europe it is a food fish. Elsewhere it is a sport fish. The similar rudd is also widespread but its distribution is discontinuous. It feeds less near the bottom than the roach.

The related chub, 30–51 cm., with green or blue metallic flanks, prefers clean running water and lives mainly near the surface, from the British Isles through central to eastern Europe. It is, however, also found in stagnant reaches, in lakes, and even in brackish waters.

Some freshwater fishes have a fairly wide distribution but are restricted as to habitat. The dace, asp, barbel and grayling are characteristic of swift-flowing streams and rivers. Bream, silver bream, bleak and the ide or orfe are found in slow-flowing rivers.

The slim-bodied dace, bluish-green with silvery

sides, 25 cm. long, is found in western Europe. The asp, dark green on the back, 40–60 cm. long, is found in similar waters in eastern Europe, but whereas dace are fished for sport or for bait but are too bony to eat, the asp is caught extensively in traps and nets, as well as on lines, commercially. Both are found occasionally in lakes. Barbel, the fish with a poisonous roe, brown to grey-green with golden glints on the sides and head, 76 cm. long, with four sensitive barbels on the mouth, occurs locally from the British Isles through central Europe to the Danube Basin. It prefers moderately deep rivers and is mainly active by night, feeding particularly on mayfly larvae.

The grayling is a fish of northern Europe, south to the plains of Italy. Salmon-like in shape, greenish-brown to blue-green, with silver-grey flanks, 46 cm. long, it has a large, purple dorsal fin. It is one of the most beautiful of freshwater fishes and has been given names such as "Queen of the Water". The grayling has been a favourite with the connoisseur since early times. Ambrose, the bishop of Milan in the fourth century, called it the flower of fishes. It is sensitive to the environment and has become extinct in many rivers due to pollution; and it is very sensitive to injury.

The gudgeon is another fish of swiftly running waters, although also found in lakes, ponds and marshes. Usually less than 15 cm. long, it is greenish-brown with a row of indistinct, rounded spots along each flank. The gudgeon lives in shoals and feeds, like so many of these fishes, on the gravel or sandy bottom, mainly on the larvae of midges, mayfly and other insects, freshwater shrimps and

HEATHER ANGEL

The grayling prefers clear, swiftly-flowing rivers but may also occur in mountain or arctic lakes. It will eat almost anything animal that comes its way, from freshwater shrimps and insect larvae to woodlice and spiders. It has even been known to eat a shrew.

FLETCHER/NSP

Bullhead or Miller's thumb on the stony bed of a shallow stream. No more than 10 cm. long, it lives under stones and rarely shows itself except at night or when the sky is overcast.

small snails. The young fish feed on the larvae of freshwater crustaceans.

The bream, silver bream and ide all live in slow-flowing to still waters in central to northern Europe. The bream and ide are around 40–45 cm. long, the others half that size or less. All have silvery flanks and the bleak is commercially exploited in eastern Europe for its scales, used in the making of artificial pearls. The rest of the fish is used as animal food or for fertilizer. The bleak is palatable but bony, although it is used for food in some parts of Europe.

The miller's thumb or bullhead, up to 10 cm. long, lives in moderate to slow-flowing streams and rivers, sometimes in lakes, at depths less than 10 m. For most of the year the bullhead is solitary, each having its home under a stone beneath which it excavates the sand. It comes out mainly at night, to feed on insect larvae or small fishes. It is broad in front and particularly pugnacious in defence of its territory. During March to April the bullheads breed; each female lays 250 eggs, gluing them to the ceiling of the male's "home", after which he fans them with his spiny fins and guards them energetically against intruders. The stone loach, elongate, scaleless, 12·5 cm. long, with four pairs of barbels around the mouth, has a similar habitat and distribution. It is sensitive to pollution and its presence or absence is used as an indicator of river pollution.

Any other claim for the most hardy fish could justifiably be challenged on behalf of the carp. This is a native of Asia, from the Black Sea to Japan, but it has been living so long in European waters as to be accepted almost as a native. When the carp was introduced to Europe is not known, except that it was as far back as the Ancient Greeks. The wild form is yellow-green on the back, greenish-yellow to bronze-yellow on the flanks, and yellowish on the underside, with two pairs of barbels on each side at the corners of the mouth. The average size is 51 cm. long and 3 kg weight, but weights of 19·8 kg. or more have been reliably recorded. Carp may live for fifteen years in the wild but when protected in ponds they have achieved fifty to seventy years and, in the lakes of Fontainebleau, are said to have lived for 400 years.

Carp do best in shallow, sunny waters with a muddy bottom and abundant water plants, in slow-running rivers of lowland plains, and in lakes and large ponds. They grub in the mud with the protrusible mouth for insect larvae, crustaceans and pond snails.

Probably the baffling difficulty encountered in trying to describe the fishes of Europe in a brief space is that there is nothing clear-cut about their habitats. A fish may typically live in a moderately fast stream, under an overhanging bank and near the bottom. Yet it may be found in other situations, as well as in lakes or even marshes. Perhaps the most troublesome species of all is that delectable fish the European trout. It is not only variable in colour and habitat but also in behaviour. Consequently, it is known by three names: brown, lake, and sea trout. The brook and rainbow trout are introductions from North America.

The brown trout is small and dark, lives in small rivers or pools, weighs up to 8 kg. and is non-migratory. The lake trout is larger and paler, lives in the larger rivers and lakes and may be migratory. The sea trout is silvery, up to 1·5 m. long and 14 kg. weight, and distinctly migratory, breeding in rivers but going to sea to feed, as far as 400 miles from the coast.

The trout is shaped like a salmon, except that the angle of the jaw reaches well past the hind margin of the eye, and although the general colour is variable the distinguishing feature is the black and red spots on the gill-covers and flanks, the red spots being usually light ringed.

Adult trout feed on small fishes, crustaceans and insect larvae. They also eat winged insects, the classic example being the mayfly, so that an account of this insect is inseparable from a discussion of rivers. Although called mayfly, there are a number of species so that one or other may be seen swarming during June or July as well. The larvae will have been living on the bottom of the river for a year. Then with weather conditions right, they swarm to the surface or creep out on to a rock or a water plant. The skin of the back splits and the adult struggles out. This is, however, the first stage in the process of growing up, for mayflies differ from all other insects in having two post-larval moults before reaching maturity.

The larva of the mayfly, and of other related insects, is preferably called a nymph. From the nymph steps out a subimago (sub-adult) which is winged and flies to the nearest bush. There the skin splits again and out comes the imago, the perfect or adult mayfly. After its wings have expanded and dried, the adult takes to the wing, on its nuptial flight, after which the females lay their eggs, in hundreds or thousands, according to the species, in the water, to provide next year's flight of mayfly; within hours they are dead.

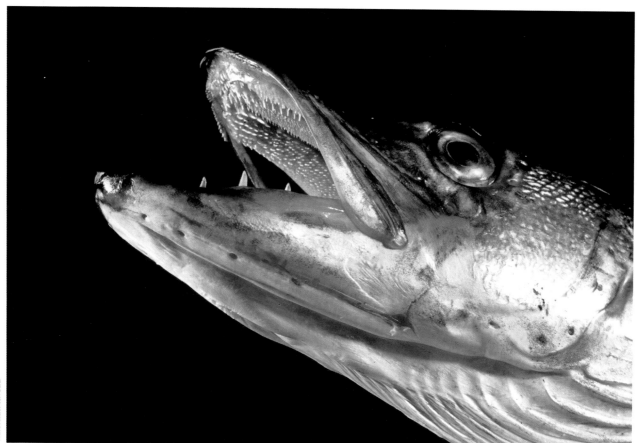

The mouth of the pike bristles with teeth, even the palate being well supplied with them; the longest teeth of this fish-eating predator are in the lower jaw. Adults feed mainly on other fish, including young pike, but will also take frogs, newts, even occasionally water birds and mammals.

Right: The stump-tailed, long-billed kingfisher feeds mainly on small fishes but takes water beetles and dragonfly larvae as well. It catches these by dropping on them from an overhanging perch or after a short hover over the water.

The life-span of the adult mayfly has been described as a fugitive one, a few hours, a day or at most several days. The larval life, by contrast, is up to three years. This brief appearance of the adults, in their hundreds of thousands, provides food for birds and fishes.

So is produced one of the annual, spectacular sights of the river. The bushes, trees, fences or boulders on either bank of the river are decorated with the dried skins of the subimagos, each with its three tails. Over the water dance the mayflies, for a few hours, or a few days at most. Swallows and martins snatch them on the wing. Those dropping into the water to lay, as some species of mayfly do, or dropping dead on to the surface, are snapped up by fishes, especially trout. Even a large trout, that normally feeds on other fishes, will rise to the surface to snap a mayfly.

The dipper is a starling-sized, wren-like bird, with short wings and short tail, living in clear fast-flowing streams all over Europe. Brown with a white bib, it flits over rocks and boulders, walking or flying in and out of water, and seemingly walking along the bottom of the river. The dipper is the only perching bird to lead an aquatic life, more like a fish, and it feeds on the same foods as many freshwater fish, such as insect larvae like caddis-worms, stonefly and dragonfly larvae. It will also take small fishes.

The diet sheet of the dipper is not unlike that of the kingfisher. This, one of the most dazzling of European birds, is usually seen as a blur of colour as it flies low over a river or lake. It also feeds on fishes and insect larvae, captured by plunging into water, seizing its prey, then flying up to the surface and into the air again. A kingfisher sits patiently on a perch, such as a twig overhanging the water, until it sees something moving in the water, or it may check in flight, hover and dive, to seize a fish with its long dagger-like bill. When examined at rest the kingfisher is seen to be iridescent blue or green on the upperparts, with a chestnut front, red legs and white patches on the neck.

A chapter on rivers would seem empty without some reference to ducks, and it is natural to associate these birds with rivers. Yet careful analysis of their habits shows that the usual habitats for ducks, other than sea ducks, are lakes and marshes. Sometimes out of the breeding season some ducks are seen on quiet rivers. Even so, the most common is the mallard and that usually keeps to the less fast-

The water vole is called a water rat in most European languages, but apart from being inoffensive compared with the true rat it has the usual vole characteristics. The muzzle is blunt, the ears are small and almost hidden in the fur and the eyes are small.

Left: Female mute swan on her nest among reeds with her mate swimming in the foreground. The male gathers rotting vegetation and carries it to her as she builds her nest, thereafter remaining in attendance when she is incubating.

flowing rivers and then keeps near the banks. Swans are more likely to be seen on rivers and being larger, with more powerful legs, they can swim against all but the strongest currents. For ordinary purposes, a swan must keep to shallow water, where it feeds by dipping its neck or up-ending to pluck submerged water plants.

Relatively few mammals have exploited the riverine habitat. The rat-sized water vole favours slow-flowing rivers and also lakes, feeding on water vegetation with a little animal food, mainly molluscs. It is widespread in Europe, from the tundra to the Mediterranean, but absent from the southern Balkans and southern Italy. Its place is taken in Iberia and much of France by the south-western water vole, and a smaller race of it is found in central Europe, especially in the Alps, living well away from water and burrowing very like a mole.

The water shrew is, like other insectivores, very active and quick in its movements. When it enters water, air is trapped in its fur making it look like a silvery bubble. Although it shares with the common shrew the long sensitive snout, small eyes and ears hidden in the fur, it can be readily distinguished by the sharp line where the black or dark-brown fur of the back meets the white of its underside. Each of its toes is fringed with bristles converting the feet into effective paddles. A row of bristles along the underside of the tail forms an effective keel. The water shrew is yet another predator on water insects and freshwater shrimps, and it occasionally eats fish. The northern water shrew ranges from the tundra to the Mediterranean region, but is not found in the lowlands in the latter. The southern water shrew lives in mountains in western Europe but on the plains of eastern Europe.

The Pyrenean desman is even better adapted to an aquatic life than the smaller water shrew. The desman is 12 cm. long with a tail 14 cm. long. Its tail is fringed with hairs and is used as a rudder. Its hind feet are webbed and all the toes are fringed with hairs. The long spatulate snout has nostrils on the upper surface which are valved. The coat is waterproof. Desmans feed on aquatic invertebrates in the fast-flowing mountain streams and in clear millstreams and canals in the Pyrenees and the north-western third of Iberia.

The desman is one of a number of species of animals, including some insects, that are restricted or almost restricted to the Iberian peninsula. Another is the Spanish moon moth, the larva of which feeds on the maritime pine in Spain. It extends slightly into southern France. The barrier of the Pyrenees cuts off Iberia from the rest of Europe, biologically speaking, as the sea cuts off the British Isles.

The two super-predators of the rivers of Europe are the mink and the otter, and both offer examples of a disappearing species. The habitat of the European mink is the rivers and streams of the coniferous and the broad-leaved forest zones and the rivers of southern Russia as far as the Caucasus, wherever there is thick undergrowth. It is a medium-sized member of the weasel family, with a dark brown fur which, although used commercially, is of inferior quality to that of the American mink. So although the European mink has been killed in large numbers for its fur, the greater menace to it is its American cousin. This was brought to Europe to be farmed for its pelt and everywhere individuals have escaped, gone feral and are spreading. In addition the American mink has been deliberately released in Russia for the sake of its fur. Mink feed on rodents, especially water voles, but also take a wide variety of other aquatic animals, such as fish, frogs, newts, crayfish, molluscs and ducks.

It is not usual to give mink the opportunity to bathe on mink farms, yet a captive mink, if

BURTON/COLEMAN

The water shrew, the largest of the European shrews, but still only 18 cm. long including the tail, is an adept swimmer. Each toe is fringed with hairs converting the feet to paddles and the tail has a keel of stiff hairs, making it an efficient rudder.

Right: Although it spends more of its time on land than in water, the otter is superbly adapted for swimming and diving. It has webbed feet, a waterproof fur, nostrils and ears that can be closed under water and an efficient tail for propulsion. It is a master of aquabatics.

The mink is desirable as a fur-bearing animal but it can be devastating to the inhabitants of streams. It is ironical that man went a long way to ridding the rivers of Europe of the native mink only to be the agent of introducing the American mink to them.

LINDAU/ARDEA

provided with a small pond will use it daily in a spectacular and quite surprising display of aquabatics, twisting, turning, somersaulting and swimming, all at high speed. The agility displayed is a fair indication of the menace posed to smaller wildlife and, if we are to judge from experience in Iceland, the spread and multiplication of the American mink could have a marked effect on birds, such as nesting ducks and waders.

The otter is the king of the river and like all royalty is seen but rarely, and approached less often. A master of swimming and diving and gliding easily through undergrowth, its alert senses give it advanced warning of approach. The result is that few naturalists can claim to have seen a wild otter, although anglers and water bailiffs fare better. The otter is said to be becoming rare in parts of Europe. This may be linked with pollution of the rivers or it may be because the banks of rivers are cleared and tidied up, giving the otter less cover. Perhaps it is that the rivers are being used more and their banks made noisy by people and traffic. Otters seem to be very sensitive to disturbance. Or it may be that its rarity is more apparent than real, an escape to lonely places away from disturbance.

It seems unlikely that hunting has had any real effect on the numbers of otters, but equally unlikely that hunting otters can be justified except as a measure of local control, for example on a salmon river. Their food is mainly fish, and usually only diseased or sick fishes are caught, of which eels seem to be a favourite. Crayfish are another favoured food item.

The Sea and its harvest

Gannets are large, white sea-birds, 1 metre long with a wing-span of 2 metres, that nest in colonies usually on small offshore islands. Two-thirds of the world's breeding population nests around the British Isles. They catch fish by diving vertically down from a height of anything up to 30 metres.

Since Europe has such a long and remarkably indented coastline it was inevitable that a high proportion of its human inhabitants would be living near the sea, from the earliest days of human settlement of the continent. It is significant that the science of marine biology was born in Europe, with the Greek philosopher and naturalist Aristotle, and was later nurtured by a succession of Europeans to whom we owe not only the development of the Science of the Sea but also the establishment of a long string of marine biological stations.

It may well be true that man's first interest in the sea was as a source of food. Initially this interest would have been in cockles, mussels, crabs and other such animals found on the shore at ebb tide, or gathered by wading into shallow water. Then inshore fishing would have followed naturally as early man constructed his first coracles. That is, however, a matter of imaginative speculation. In due course, and here we are dealing with fact, the sea's harvest exerted a tremendous influence on the course of human history and on the development of the continent as a whole, not only because it yielded food but also because of the utilization of the sea's products as treasure in some form or another. Most obvious among these products are the many kinds of shells, but perhaps the most outstanding, certainly one of the most organized, attempts to pluck inedible treasure from the sea began when it was found that a sponge could be put to a multitude of uses.

Unfortunately, the word "sponge" has been applied to two objects, the animal and its skeleton. When the non-zoologist speaks of a sponge he refers to a coherent mass of fibres, used mainly for cleaning purposes. To the zoologist a sponge is any of 2,500 species very low in the animal scale, a few of which have a fibrous skeleton which, when cleaned of its flesh, can be used for a variety of purposes, including personal toilet.

Ernest J. J. Cresswell, in his book *Sponges*, published in the early 1920s, saw in the use of sponges an index of civilization. He pointed out that the Phoenicians, Egyptians, Greeks, Romans, Byzantines and Venetians used large numbers of sponges at the height of their civilization, and that as each civilization declined so did the use of sponges.

The properties of sponges were appreciated at least as far back as the times of the Phoenicians and Ancient Egyptians. From then sponge-fishing developed into a large industry employing thousands of people. In classical times, as today, the trade

Acorn barnacles, limpets and mussels are the commonest marine animals. They live in uncountable billions on rocky shores as well as in the sea beyond. Their larvae form an important part of the animal plankton which supports directly so many of the larger inhabitants of the sea.

WARD/NSP

was largely in the hands of the Greeks, the divers themselves being trained from infancy, and one feature of their training was to develop the ability to remain under water for a long time. It is not surprising therefore that swimming and diving should have been introduced into the first Olympic Games. What is perhaps more surprising is that with men diving daily to such depths, knowledge of the sea's inhabitants should have been so slow to accumulate. The explanation may be that when a sponge-diver is under water he has something else to occupy his mind.

Cresswell has pointed out that sponges were necessary to physicians and alchemists (later chemists) in classical times. They were also commonly used for all cleaning purposes, in certain religious rites and by the army. The best sponges were used for placing inside a soldier's knee-shields to prevent the knees being cut, and every soldier carried a sponge for drinking purposes, which explains why the Roman soldier gave a sponge soaked in vinegar to Christ during the Crucifixion.

Of the few species of sponges having a commercial value, the best are fished in the Mediterranean and especially its eastern half, although bath sponges, to use an inclusive term, of varying quality and often in relatively scanty numbers, are found in most warm seas. Sponges are, however, being replaced today by synthetic products.

Pearls are no more than the deposit laid down by an oyster around some foreign body irritating its tissues. They are another form of treasure which for centuries has been harvested from the sea-bed. The pearl-fishing industry also faces competition, from artificial pearl culture, but as with sponges

DALTON/NHPA

The edible crab lives offshore, in moderately shallow water, but is sometimes found under rocks on the shore.

A conglomerate of marine invertebrates coating the submerged rocks of the warm shallow seas. Conspicuous are the numerous small polyps and a lace-like sea-mat in the centre.

WIGHTMAN/ARDEA

The squat lobster has nothing to do with the lobsters caught as sea foods. It is related to the hermit crab, is only 5 to 7 cm. long and can commonly be seen under rocks on the shore at low-tide.

BROMHALL/ARDEA

143

the natural product can probably never be fully replaced. It is hard enough to account for the attraction a light has for a moth, but it is even more difficult to see why pearls should have attracted such universal attention and why they should command such high prices. Yet for thousands of years people have prized them highly, often investing them with magical powers.

Some of the supposed magic lay in a belief that a powder from crushed pearls restored sexual potency; and those unable to afford this particular prescription could get by on the cheaper mother-of-pearl pulverized. More important, in at least one instance the course of history has been changed because of man's lust for pearls, since it was the fame of British pearls that drew Caesar to invade and conquer Britain. That these were pearls from freshwater mussels does not alter the principle.

For a long time the biological origin of pearls was a mystery. The Ancient Greeks held that pearls were formed when lightning struck the sea. Another belief was that at certain times oysters came to the surface, opened their shells and received an angel's tear, which crystallized into a pearl.

There was an equal mystery about the origin of precious coral. Legend had it that Perseus, having overcome the Gorgon Medusa, threw her head on the shore, and the sea nymphs were so delighted with seeing the end of this winged monster that they pelted the head with bits of seaweed, for the joy of seeing them turned to stone. The legend continued, that seeds from the petrified seaweeds fell into the sea and grew into green plants which, when brought to the surface and into contact with air, turned red. This was the precious coral of the Mediterranean that has been over-fished and which today is relatively rare.

It may be that somewhere out of this improbable idea the belief arose, by the usual alchemy of the human mind, that the precious coral had magical or medicinal properties, that it was suitable, therefore, to be made into jewellery, and that it was efficacious in some way to have this coral jewellery for personal adornment. Yet this cannot be the whole story, for the Ancient Britons, who could have had no knowledge of it as a natural product, readily traded with the Gauls for the red coral, and for many centuries since it has had a value in the world's market, for trinkets as well as, at one time, a medicine (when powdered). Even now, in some parts of the world, coral necklaces are still regarded as having a therapeutic value.

The Ancient Greeks believed the seas were ruled by gods attended by demi-gods, or Tritons. A Triton was pictured as half-man, half-fish blowing a great twisted sea-shell to raise or to calm the waves. The use of a shell, or conch, as a trumpet or a horn is only one of the many useful adaptations made possible by the wide variety of shapes and sizes found in marine molluscs. Others are made into lamps or ornate dishes, trays and similar decorative as well as useful objects. One of the largest conch shells, known as the bailer shell (Cymbium amphora), has long been used in primitive canoes, for bailing.

It is perhaps unnecessary to recall that oysters, clams, mussels, winkles and other shellfish have provided a source of income to those who fish them, and have fed the hungry and satisfied the desires of gastronomes for many long centuries. The heaped banks of oyster shells alone, at places on the coasts, tell only part of the story. Caches of oyster shells are constantly being unearthed on the sites of ancient middens, telling of the widespread and long-established taste for what some gastronomes consider the king of shellfish. But the desire to gather marine molluscs goes well beyond the need for food, the love of oysters, or the commercial exploitation of mother-of-pearl. It takes us into the realm of the collector.

In the seas off the Channel Islands is found a beautiful limpet known as an ear-shell or abalone. It is less common than formerly because its flesh is tasty and it has been over-fished. Several centimetres across, its shell is ear-shaped, with an arc of small holes near one margin, through which the animal's siphon can be pushed out, and the inner surface of the shell is lined with a fine iridescent mother-of-pearl. It is only one of many species found in warm waters throughout the world, and the most famous is the red abalone of the Pacific coast of North America.

Another gastropod mollusc early achieved a high market value but for an entirely different reason. Probably the first dye that could be permanently fixed in wool and linen was the famous Tyrian purple, named after the city of Tyre, in Phoenicia, on the eastern coast of the Mediterranean. The murex whelk (Murex trunculus), of the Mediterranean, gives out from certain glands a brownish fluid which on exposure to air oxidizes to a rich purple. The Phoenicians boiled the whelk and by various processes purified the dye. After the decline of Phoenicia both Greece and Rome discovered the secret, and wool dyed purple continued to realize very high prices until an edict was issued prohibiting its use by any but the imperial family in Rome. After that the industry died, and the secret of making the purple was lost until the Renaissance.

Another kind of shell, also avidly collected but for a totally different purpose, is so unlike the conventional shell that it is called bone, cuttlebone. It is always something of a surprise, to those who learn it for the first time, that octopuses, cuttle and squid are molluscs, related to snails, oysters and clams. This is partly because of their size and their agility and also because they appear to be without shells. But just as a slug is no more than a snail devoid of a shell, or, as in some species of slugs, with a shell inside the body instead of outside, so the octopus is a mollusc devoid of a shell and a cuttlefish is a mollusc with its shell inside.

The Neapolitan fishermen catch cuttlefish by an unfair ruse. They capture a female and tow her behind their boat. Then, using lanterns to aid the attractiveness of their bait, they catch the males that follow the female. The flesh of the cuttlefish is less highly regarded than that of the octopus and squid, but fishing for cuttle brings lucrative side-products. The cuttlefish is named *Sepia officinalis*, and part of its defence mechanism is to give out ink from a sac within the body. Placed in a tank of water and then disturbed, a cuttlefish will soon turn the water to blackness with its ink. Dried ink-sacs from the cuttlefish furnish the sepia used in water colours. In former times they furnished the ink for writing. That is, however, not the end. Its shell, or cuttlebone, is used for tooth-powders and for polishing, where a soft abrasive is needed; and cuttlebone, ground up, supplies an excellent

antacid for indigestion. Today, however, there is probably more cuttlebone used for cage-birds than for any other purpose.

The eating of fish, either raw, cooked or preserved, usually by salting or smoking, must go back to very early times. Much of the fish must, to begin with, have been freshwater species, and in large parts of the world today, in regions distant from a coastline, freshwater fishes are exploited largely to the exclusion of marine fishes. Even so, the sea fisheries have had and still have an importance that is difficult to overstate. These sea fisheries lie principally in the north temperate zone and for the most part between latitudes 40° to 70° north.

A large part of the world's harvest from this source is represented by the fishing industries of Great Britain, France, Spain, Norway and Russia. The number of species fished in this area is far fewer than in warmer seas but their populations are far greater and more concentrated and fishing is therefore more economic.

The fish are caught on the continental shelves. In Europe these extend as a narrow band along the coasts of Portugal, Spain and south-western France, then take a wide sweep to the west around the British Isles. The North Sea and much of

The cuttlefish as a living animal is a most unfamiliar sight, although it is numerous enough in the sea. It swims near the bottom hunting shrimps and prawns, which it seizes with a pair of long arms. When not in use these are withdrawn within the circle of the eight tentacles around its mouth.

the Bay of Biscay are less than 180 m. deep. A slightly deeper shelf extends to Iceland and along the coast of Norway to the arctic coast of Russia. Together they form the largest and richest fishing area in the world, rivalled only by the eastern seaboard of North America, including the famous cod banks of Newfoundland.

The future expansion of the world's fisheries depends to a large extent on our knowledge of fish migrations. This applies especially to the pelagic species. We need to know the routes they take, the times they appear in certain places, and the reasons why they sometimes fail to put in an appearance in places where they are expected.

The migrations of the tunny afford a suitable example to illustrate this. Scientists have long had their eyes on this problem, beginning with Aristotle, who noted tunny migrating into the Black Sea through the Bosphorus. They returned to the Aegean Sea in September; and Aristotle noted that on both journeys the tunny hugged the shore on their left-hand side. His theory was that the fish were blind in one eye.

Much later still it was thought that the tunny living in the Mediterranean passed through the Strait of Gibraltar, moved northwards past the Iberian peninsula, past Ireland, and then diverged north of Scotland, some going to the waters off Norway and some turning south into the North Sea. The latest information suggests there is not one migration but four, on the part of four different groups of tunny, all belonging to one species. There is one group moving from the Aegean to the Black Sea and back, one from Sicily to the coast of Tunis and back, one from off the north-west coast of Africa to Portugal and back, and one from the north-west of Spain to Norway and the North Sea and back. The four lines of movement almost make up sections of a continuous line from the Black Sea to the North Sea.

One reason for the regular journeys, represented by the movements given in detail above, is that the fishes are moving from a feeding ground to a spawning ground. Consequently the migrating shoals are made up of large individuals only, the young tunny remaining inshore until they are mature.

It is more than likely that the tunny, in their migrations, are either following their food species or moving with water which is around their optimum temperature. Léon Bertin favoured the latter theory when he included tunny with the mackerel, herring, pilchard, anchovy, plaice and

cod, as fishes that move about without changing their environment. The other type of migratory movement is from salt to fresh water, as with the salmon, sea trout, sturgeon and sea lamprey, which feed in the sea but move into fresh water to spawn, or, like the eel, live in fresh water but spawn in the sea.

The mackerel can be taken as the first example of a fish that migrates without changing its environment. Mackerel leave the surface waters at the end of October, swimming down to the sea-bed to depths of up to 186 m., mainly along the edge of the continental shelf. There they concentrate in hollows and troughs in the sea-bed. Towards the end of December they spread out over the sea-floor to feed on small crustaceans, worms and small fishes. In late January or early February they rise, as the warm layers of water rise, to the surface and begin their spawning migrations. Moving slowly, mackerel converge on the Celtic Sea, the area south of Ireland and west of the English Channel.

Here enormous shoals of mackerel spawn, from March to June, each female laying from half a million to a million eggs, egg-laying being protracted over a long period of time. The eggs are pelagic at first, floating for two days then sinking halfway down, staying a few days, then settling on the bottom where they hatch. The spawning ground is in a wide crescent 100 miles west of the Scillies. After spawning, the mackerel move slowly back towards the coasts. During this time they feed on animal plankton, especially on the copepods *Calanus* and *Anomalocera*. In June they break up into small shoals, now feeding on young herrings, sprats and sand-eels, found in the shallower bays along the coast. Towards the end of October they swim down to concentrate once more in the troughs on the sea-bed in deep waters.

The herring ranges from the coast of Maine, in the north-eastern United States, to Nova Scotia and Newfoundland, Greenland, Iceland, the Barents Sea, along the coast of Norway and southwards to the northern part of the Bay of Biscay. At one time it was believed that herring made extensive migrations. Then came the discovery that the species is divided into well-marked local races which differ in the number of vertebrae, in the maximum length attained, and in the age at which they reach sexual maturity.

The complete picture of the herring's movements has yet to be worked out but enough is known to show that there is no long migration from Iceland through the North Sea and into the English

Mackerel and haddock in the fisherman's basket, two of the more favoured of Europe's food fishes.

Red gurnard and pout are marine fishes often taken in the trawl in European seas. Neither is of great commercial value, and the pout is usually processed into fish-meal.

Channel. Instead, local races appear in shoals at different times at successive points along this route, so giving an appearance of a migration.

It has been said that wherever the shoals of herrings came in towards the coast of Norway, there sprang up a fishing village. The same is probably true for Scotland and elsewhere. The villages later became towns. In addition there are towns that were deliberately founded to cater for the fishing. Hamburg was founded in A.D. 809 by Charlemagne, as a herring port, and the Normans, descendants of the Vikings, founded Ostend, Dunkirk, Etaples, Dieppe and Fécamp, for the same purpose. From Norway and Belgium to the coast of Prussia were many free cities and small states engaged in general trade, and they needed armed escorts for their merchandise. In the thirteenth century they banded together to sail their great merchant fleets in convoy, for protection. They became known as the Hanseatic League, with headquarters at Lübeck.

The League monopolized almost the whole of Europe's export trade and for two centuries was the dominating influence in northern Europe. Its wealth was based on the Baltic herring. Its ships carried herrings from the Baltic ports and brought

back wool, wine, timber and other merchandise. Then suddenly the Baltic herring was gone, the reason for which is still not certain. At about the same time the Dutch began to export herrings fished in English waters. By 1610 they employed an estimated 3,000 ships and 50,000 people. Friction arose between Holland and England, because the latter wanted to extract tribute for herrings taken in her waters. This led incidentally to the foundation of the Royal Navy and to the Anglo-Dutch war of 1652–54, in which England wrested sea power from Holland.

No single fish has had more influence on the course of human history or has existed in such great abundance. Herrings have been systematically fished for centuries, and in modern times have been caught at an estimated 3,000 million a year throughout their range. Wherever the herring fishers went there was trouble between nations, ending in the Russo-Japanese war of 1902, which arose from a Japanese claim to the herrings off the Russian island of Sakhalin.

Beside the herring fishery the sardine trade is relatively insignificant, yet it has represented a lucrative venture over a long period. The species known as *Sardina pilchardus* is called a sardine when young and a pilchard when mature. The first forms the basis of an extensive canning industry in France, Spain and Portugal; the second is best known for the pilchard fishery which formerly flourished off Cornwall. The pilchards are caught by drift-nets and seines. In drift-netting the nets are shot at sunset, the nets being fastened end-to-end, the one end being attached by a rope to the

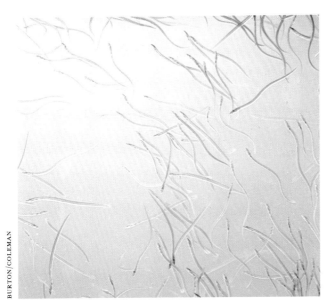

Elvers migrating upstream. Freshwater eels migrate to mid-Atlantic to spawn and do not return. Their larvae make the return journey, taking nearly three years to reach the coasts of Europe. There they metamorphose and as elvers swarm up the rivers in incredible numbers.

Herring gulls are so named from their habit of following the herring fleets and feeding on the fish offal thrown overboard. Their food at other times is many kinds of marine animals, of which one-fifth is fish, and carrion and ships' refuse.

bow of a boat so that nets and boat drift with the tide.

The European eel, strictly speaking, should have no place in a chapter on the sea, since it spends most of its life in fresh water. Yet it originates in the ocean and returns to it. It also furnishes what is probably the classic example of aquatic migration, if only for the tremendous research that has gone into the attempt to solve its mysteries. The story has been told so often that only brief mention need be made of its history: how Aristotle over two thousand years ago pointed out that neither ripe ova nor milt had been found in an eel; how Pliny, the Roman naturalist, declared eels had no sex but rubbed themselves against rocks, the pieces of skin rubbed off becoming young eels; and how later people believed eels came from horsehairs thrown into the water.

Even in the early years of this century all that was known was that in spring shoals of elvers, or young eels, 75 mm. long, made their way up the rivers, and that in autumn large numbers of adult eels returned to the sea. In the second half of the eighteenth century, small leaf-shaped fishes were found in the Mediterranean and in British waters, and these were given the name of *Leptocephalus*. They were presumed to be larval fishes representing a distinct group of fishes. Towards the end of the nineteenth century they were recognized to be larval eels, but it was then presumed that eels bred in deep water near the coast. Then came the famous researches of the Dane, Johannes Schmidt, who, patiently over many years, tracked the leptocephali on their long journey, which occupies nearly three years, from the Sargasso Sea to the coasts of Europe, where they metamorphose into elvers and then enter the estuaries to migrate up the rivers.

When the elvers swarm up the rivers in spring they are caught all over Europe for use as human food. Despite these inroads into their numbers, and the toll taken of the adult eels by man, otters, herons and other predators, enormous numbers of eels survive to make the final spawning migration. They die on their spawning grounds in mid-Atlantic and are eaten by marine predators and scavengers, their carcasses representing a large transfer of nutrient material from fresh waters to the oceans. If no more, this underlines the intimate link that exists between the economy of a continent and that of the sea.

The Atlantic salmon, by contrast with the eel, feeds at sea and brings nutritive materials back to the rivers. Salmon come up the rivers of Europe to spawn. As the young salmon grow they migrate down the rivers to the sea, where they may travel up to 1,000 miles from their river of origin, feeding for several years before maturing and returning to their natal rivers to spawn and, usually, die. This fish, now a luxury in parts of Europe, has had a chequered history. There was a time when salmon was so plentiful it represented a cheap food and apprentices in Britain rebelled if given salmon to eat more than twice a week. Now many salmon rivers have been polluted with factory effluents or poisoned by pesticides washed into the water from farmlands.

During the thirteenth to the eighteenth century, in Spain, 10,000 salmon were caught every day. By 1949 only 3,000 were being caught in a year, the result of over-fishing, poaching, the damming of rivers for irrigation and pollution by waste from factories. The story for France is similar but in

Norway the salmon fishery has improved, also in Sweden, by the use of hatcheries.

Today, the European seas have been more or less cleared of whales and even the smaller dolphins and porpoises are a sufficiently unusual sight that they always arouse interest. At one time they contributed largely to the economy of Europe.

The earliest record we have of man's interest in whales is in a Stone Age drawing scratched on rock at Røddøy, in northern Norway, and believed to date from about 2200 B.C. The Norwegians, with their long coastline and narrow mountainous hinterland, must always have had an incentive to draw their food from the sea, and there is a record of whaling, possibly of the North Atlantic right whales, at Tromsö in A.D. 890. However, the first to pursue the large whales systematically were the Basques, and in the twelfth century whaling was well established as an industry along the shores of the Bay of Biscay. Some of the names still used in the industry, such as harpoon, are of Basque origin, although "whale" itself is from the Norwegian *hval* and Anglo-Saxon *hwail,* words believed to be related to "wheel", which may be expressive of the way whales turn when at the surface.

Analysis of the records suggests that the total catch of whales for twenty Basque villages between 1517 and 1617 was short of a thousand, an average of less than half a whale a year per village, an insignificant figure when contrasted with the inroads into the stocks of whales in the twentieth century. Yet even this small amount of slaughter seems to have been harmful to the stocks of Biscayan right whales that habitually entered the inshore waters of the Basque coastland during winter and early spring. By the middle of the sixteenth century the whales had become so scarce that the Basque whalers were having to go far afield for their catches, even to Newfoundland. The first English expedition to Spitzbergen, in 1711, included Basque whalers, who held a virtual monopoly of the necessary knowledge and skill. At Spitzbergen the whales were found in immense numbers. They were unafraid and were taken in large numbers, bulls, cows and calves alike, with comparative ease. By 1720 the Spitzbergen area was cleared of whales. One area of the Arctic after another was visited, exploited, and drained of its whales.

We may assume that in prehistoric times the meat was the most important part taken, although it is inconceivable that the rest was wholly wasted; and in various places and at other times, even down to today, whale meat has been and still is an important product. After the meat, lamp oil and whalebone were the chief products. When steel and elastic were unknown, whalebone was important, at one time fetching as much as £2,250 a ton. The whalebone was used in the manufacture of brushes, for fishing rods, and in any article in which supporting frames were needed. As other forms of lighting came into use, whale oil went out of demand, and as light steel and later plastics were introduced, the need for whalebone declined.

In more modern times the greatest single product of whaling has been the use of oil in the manufacture of margarine. Whale oil has also been used for making soap and as a drying oil in paint. Inferior grades of the oil are used for tanning.

During the eleventh to the fourteenth centuries there was, it appears, a fair traffic in whale meat in western Europe, and it was regarded as a special delicacy. Today it finds little favour in Europe outside Norway, but much more use is being made of whale meat as pet food.

The seals are confined mainly to the northern waters of Europe. With the exception of the common seal which ranges from Finmark to Oporto, and the monk seal of the Mediterranean and Black Seas, the British Isles form their southern

Kittiwake with two young at the nest on a cliff ledge. Kittiwakes usually keep well out at sea, and are found especially over the northern fishing grounds. They nest on cliffs along the coast of Norway and around much of the British Isles, with a few colonies on the Brest peninsula of France.

The lesser Rorqual or Minke whale *Balaenoptera Acutorostrata* is cosmopolitan and can be seen in European seas. It is not infrequently stranded on the coasts. Fully grown it reaches ten metres in length and is distinguished by the white bands on its flippers.

Grey seal pups on a rocky shore. The grey seal is found on the coasts of Atlantic Canada, Greenland and Iceland, and on the coasts of Europe from Britanny to Norway and the Baltic. Their greatest concentration is around the British Isles.

Above, right: The fulmar petrel ranges throughout the Arctic and adjacent seas. During the last century fulmars off St Kilda have spread in a spectacular fashion southwards around the British Isles, a population explosion due to feeding on offal from fishing and whaling fleets.

Below, right: The black guillemot is a much smaller bird than the common guillemot, and differs slightly in its range, which is mainly the coastlines of Ireland, western Scotland, Scandinavia, Finland and Iceland. It feeds closer inshore than the common guillemot, taking shrimps, prawns, crabs, molluscs and worms as well as fish.

limit. The ringed seal is the commonest seal of Arctic seas but there is a large population in the Baltic Sea. Ringed seals bear their single pups on the frozen sea, sometimes hiding them in a lair under the snow. The grey or Atlantic seal, distinguished by its "Roman" nose, also breeds in the Baltic, as well as around the coasts of Norway to the White Sea and around the British Isles. The pups are born in crowded colonies, usually on islands or on rocky shores, except in the Baltic where they are dropped on the ice. They are suckled for three weeks, becoming very fat on their mother's rich milk, and are then deserted. After shedding their white natal coats they put to sea to fend for themselves. The widespread common seal is more of an inshore animal than the grey seal. It gathers to breed in estuaries and sea lochs and sometimes penetrates many miles up rivers. The pups are sometimes born in the water and can swim well from birth. Their white coat is shed before they are born.

Europe's seals are true seals of the family Phocidae, distinguished from the eared seals—the fur seals and sealions—of the family Otariidae by the lack of an external earflap and the inability to turn the hindflippers forward. They cannot bound over the ground like a sealion but have to crawl laboriously on their bellies. European waters have two rare visitors from the Arctic, the bearded seal and the walrus. The walrus belongs to a family of its own, the Odobenidae. At one time it was a quite common visitor but it was hunted for its hide and tusks. It is still seen at rare intervals on British and Norwegian coasts.

Collared doves, the birds that have found their way across Europe during the present century, furnishing scientists with a well documented history of how an animal species can spread.

North of the mountain ranges of southern Europe the retreating ice-cap left more than half the continent bare and open to invasion by plants and animals. Much of this re-colonization came from the east, from Asia, and the easiest route, especially for non-flying animals, lay through the steppes corridor lying to the south of the Urals and to the north of the Caspian and Black Seas. Plants, with wind-borne seeds, and flying animals, such as bats and birds, would find hills and mountains like, for example, the Urals, less of a barrier. That such invasions did take place is implicit in the similarities between the faunas of Asia and Europe.

Species may spread from the pressures of high population numbers, coupled with a natural tendency of some individuals to wander. They also spread, and are more influenced to do so, by finding a new source of food. Naturally, the history of invasions that took place prior to the historical period, or in the early part of the historical period, before objective documentation was made, has to be inferred. So do their causes. There is, however, an early invasion which can be inferred with a fair degree of certainty because the cause is fairly obvious. This is the spread of the house mouse *Mus musculus*.

It is generally agreed that the house mouse was originally native to the steppes of central Asia and probably also the Mediterranean region. It lived in the countryside, a wild mouse in every respect, independent of man. Some of its descendants still live like that, in their original, native areas. Others of their descendants battened on man, after he had begun to grow grain crops, and as man the cereal-grower settled across Europe the symbiotic, some

prefer to say parasitic, mouse destined to be named the house mouse, went with him. These symbiotic or parasitic house mice became bigger than the truly wild progenitor and their tails grew longer. In Europe today they are represented by three sub-species. West of a line from Hamburg to Venice lives the sub-species *M. m. domesticus*. East of this line lives the sub-species *M. m. musculus*. Throughout the Mediterranean is a symbiotic (or parasitic) sub-species, *M. m. brevirostris*.

The house mouse is adaptable, even enterprising. It is adaptable in being able to thrive on a variety of foods and to make its home in a wide range of places. Adaptability is one of the secrets of colonization of new areas. Some house mice have even adapted to living in cold meat stores, growing longer fur, becoming meat-eaters and nesting in the frozen carcasses. Many more have been carried by ships all over the world, even to the continent of Antarctica.

Comparison is inevitable between the history of the house mouse and two other rodents, the black or ship rat and the brown or common rat. All three have lessons to teach us, in biology, in ecology, ethology and zoogeography. Obviously it is not possible to discuss every aspect of their complicated progress in detail here. Nevertheless, the bare bones of the story are still illuminating.

The black rat was the first to spread across Europe. Much of the early history of that spread is lost in the mists of antiquity, so it can only be etched in. Zoologists are agreed that the original home of the black rat was central Asia. Little is known about it until the twelfth century. Certainly, it was unknown to the Ancient Greeks and Romans.

The early history of the spread of the house mouse from Asia is not known. Not all members of the species have become 'house' mice, some strains being found still living in the wild.

Black rat on a sack of grain. One of the worst features of infestation by rats is not so much the amount of stored foods they eat but the far greater amount they spoil by contaminating it.

MARKHAM/COLEMAN

BURTON/COLEMAN

Giraldus Cambrensis was the first to record its presence in the west, in 1188, when he wrote of *mures* swarming in vast numbers in Ireland. He described them as "the larger mice that are commonly called rats" that nibbled the books of the bishop St Yvor, who cursed them and so expelled them from Ireland.

Tradition has it that the black rat was first brought to Europe in the ships of the Crusaders returning from the wars in the Holy Land. Reality has it that in the fourteenth century Europe was struck by the Black Death, the pestilential plague (bubonic) that ravaged Europe killing in places ninety per cent of the human population. The plague was carried by the rat flea, and the wide incidence of it is sufficient indication of how widespread and numerous the rat had become. Whether the rodent had spread through the steppes corridor or purely by ships will never be known. Probably both contributed.

Six centuries later the brown rat burst upon the European scene in what must have been a similar manner. One of the firm records is of its arrival in Denmark in 1716, in ships coming from Russia. It seems to have reached Ireland about 1722 and England in 1760, a strange coincidence that both the black and the brown rat should have reached Ireland before they reached England. Transit in ships was not, however, the main cause of the spread through Europe. Peter Pallas, the celebrated naturalist, recorded hordes of brown rats crossing the Volga in 1727 after an earthquake. The Volga is one of the rivers traversing the steppes corridor.

It may have been pure coincidence that the earthquake preceded the invasion by the rats, for in a short while they overran the whole of western Russia. What we have learned subsequently is that brown rats are liable to travel in swarms after being disturbed. One of the early reports in Britain, following the brown rats' arrival, told of rats eating standing wheat while the farm labourers were reaping it. In more modern times, brown rats have been seen leaving a wheatfield as the combine harvester cut the wheat. Two things have been noticeable, then. The first is that the rats are so tame they take no notice of people. Presumably they have been among the wheat for months and represent a generation that has grown up without reason to recognize humans as enemies. The second is that the rats, having fed on whatever is available, then move off in droves, not to the next feeding ground, but covering long distances before settling down to feed again. It is probably this trick of behaviour that carried them across Europe in a short time.

The most remarkable comparable instance in modern times of an invader, or colonizer, is the collared dove. It also is of Asiatic origin, and its movements probably give a clue to the causes of the mouse and rat invasions: that they were following food. The collared dove seems to have been favoured by the Turks who, apparently, construed its call as *Allah-hu-akbar* (Allah is the greatest). It seems to have been well known to the Ancient Greeks who invented a legend about it, that a domestic servant who was paid only 18 paras a year—a para being a Turkish coin worth about a twelfth of a penny—appealed to the gods to let the world know of her miserable plight. Zeus responded by creating the collared dove, ordaining it should cry *decaocto, decaocto* (eighteen) for evermore.

The facts are less romantic but equally startling. The collared dove was introduced into extreme south-eastern Europe from Asia Minor by the Turks, and there it stayed until 1835, when it turned up in Bulgaria. Then, in 1912, it appeared in Belgrade. After that its spread was rapid. It reached Hungary in 1930, Austria in 1943, Venice in 1944, Germany in 1946 and Holland in 1948. The first breeding record for the British Isles was in 1955, since when it has spread and multiplied rapidly.

The natural foods of the collared dove are seeds, berries and other fruit. The secret of its spread is that it has taken to settling wherever grain is put down for poultry or wherever grain is spilt, on farms or where grain is loaded or off-loaded.

Few animal species can equal the adaptability and enterprise of the brown rat, which have enabled the species to spread decisively over a large part of the world. As if raiding buildings were not enough, brown rats not uncommonly scavenge the seashore at low-tide, especially at night.

It is axiomatic that a species will spread to occupy an ecological niche left vacant by the dying out or killing off of another species. This is often the case but it is not invariably so. Britain is plagued today by the grey squirrel from North America. Throughout the nineteenth century grey squirrels had been liberated in various parts of England and Wales. In some instances they became pests locally; in two instances they flourished for a while and then died out; in no instance did they spread far from the point where they were liberated. Then, during the years 1890 to 1914, further groups of grey squirrels were liberated, one group near Dumbarton in Scotland, the others in the southern half of England, notably at Woburn Park in Bedfordshire, and in London's Regent's Park and in Richmond Park, Surrey. Today they are abundant throughout most of England, and the pattern of their spread from isolated centres, both from those mentioned and others not mentioned, is of a period during which the numbers build up but with little extension of the range, followed by a bursting out and spreading rapidly and far. This can only happen provided the food supply is adequate.

It has often been argued that the grey squirrel drove out the native red squirrel because the former is a more robust and aggressive animal. On the other hand, it has been suggested that disease had thinned the ranks of the red squirrel and this left a partially empty ecological niche for the grey squirrel to occupy. What is certain is that once the more active and aggressive grey squirrel occupies an area there is little chance that the red squirrel will be able to stage a recovery in it.

Arguments one way or the other tend to be conflicting. Perhaps the best that can be said is that if a species is sufficiently adaptable, enterprising or robust, it will probably flourish once it has colonized new ground. This is likely to be true whether it finds an empty ecological niche or fashions a new one for itself. An example of the latter is possibly to be found in the musk-rat.

This is a rodent, up to 40 cm. long in head and body, that is found throughout the forested areas of North America where there are slow-flowing rivers. It carries a valuable fur, and half a century ago it was imported into Europe to be ranched or to be deliberately set free in marshy areas to provide a source of income. Many musk-rats escaped from the ranches and they and those deliberately set free sometimes became a nuisance in the Low Countries, France, Germany, Hungary, Czechoslovakia, Po-

land and Finland by burrowing into the banks of rivers and boring through dams, creating marshes where grassland existed before. From 1927 to 1937 the musk-rat became feral in Britain, so the authorities, alarmed at the damage it was doing to agriculture, launched a successful campaign to exterminate it. The musk-rat is a close relative of the European water vole, and where the two overlap the musk-rat pushes out the smaller water vole, ousting it from its ecological niche.

Another large American rodent has become established in Europe, partly by design and partly by accident. This is the coypu, larger than the musk-rat and smaller than the beaver. Like the beaver it can burrow into banks or build homes of piles of vegetation but it lives in marshes rather than rivers. A native of South America, it carries a valuable fur, known as nutria. So the coypu became a desirable animal for ranching, and this was done in several places in Europe, in eastern England, France, Holland, Denmark, Germany and in eastern Europe. In some places, especially in the U.S.S.R., it has been deliberately set free in marshy places, to be harvested for fur and flesh.

The coypu does not fell trees or eat bark, like a beaver, but it damages banks and rivers and lakes and can be troublesome in eating crops such as sugar beet. Provided it can be kept within bounds it does little more than partially replace the beaver, which has disappeared from much of Europe. The main danger lies in the possibility of population explosions leading to a rapid spread, although the size of the animal will always make it vulnerable in any systematic campaign against it.

Nevertheless, there is still the example of the American mink, a small carnivore with a valuable fur. It is a medium-sized weasel that has been ranched in Scandinavia and Finland, Germany and Britain. In all these countries mink have escaped from the farms and gone feral, rapidly spreading along rivers, feeding on small rodents and also birds, especially nesting ducks and waders. The European mink was formerly widespread across Europe, from France to Finland and southern Russia, and although pockets of it are still to be found elsewhere it is now mainly in southern Russia. It is, however, a diminishing species, as a result of persecution for its fur, and for the damage it does. Even in Russia, which is the remaining stronghold of the European mink, the American mink has been farmed, and has become feral, and it has also been deliberately liberated as a commercial asset.

The coypu of South America was introduced for its fur, nutria, to parts of Europe. It is a large aquatic rodent over 1 metre long, including nearly 41 cm. of scaly, rat-like tail. The female may have a litter of 3 to 12 young that can swim a few hours after birth.

The raccoon dog has a face like a raccoon but otherwise looks like a short-legged fox. It ranges over much of Asia. In Japan it is now rare, having been hunted for its fur and flesh. Since 1928 it has been liberated in Russia and has spread westwards to Poland, Rumania, Hungary, Czechoslovakia and western Germany, and northwards to Finland, Sweden and Norway, along the rivers. Its food is small vertebrates, especially fishes, and vegetable matter, including fruit and acorns. The raccoon dog seems to do little harm, rather like the North American raccoon which has become feral in several parts of Europe.

Apart from two surprises, the remaining "aliens" are deer. The first of the "surprises" is Bennett's wallaby from Australia; it has been kept as a park animal on several estates in southern to midland England. Some of these have escaped, and in Derbyshire a moderate-sized colony became established. The second is the spiny mouse that ranges from Pakistan through Arabia to North Africa. It has become established on the islands of Crete and Cyprus, where it lives in houses, probably having reached there in cargo ships.

The imported deer are of five kinds; all were imported as park animals, and all have become

Grey squirrels were imported from North America in the nineteenth century and their numbers have now reached pest-proportions in most of Britain. With the rabbit-pest in Australia they help to underline the folly of introducing and liberating animals from other parts of the world.

feral and are breeding freely in the wild. The Chinese water deer, 55 cm. high at the shoulder, has no antlers but has long upper canine teeth. Its native home is China and Korea, among tall grasses through which it scuttles like a rabbit. There are feral populations in south-east England and in France. The Chinese muntjac—"the deer that barks like a dog"—is feral in southern and central England and France. It is only slightly larger than the water deer, has long upper canines and small two-tined antlers, and keeps very much to cover.

The white-tailed or Virginian deer, of North America, slightly smaller than the red deer, has been feral in south-west Finland since 1934. The axis deer, chital or Indian spotted deer, about the same size, has been feral since 1911 in Istria, in Yugoslavia. The sika or Japanese deer, about the size of the red deer, is feral in Ireland, Britain, France, Denmark, Germany and Austria.

Deer are pleasant animals to see in the countryside but can be damaging to crops, plantations and gardens. It is questionable whether a densely settled continent can afford to have five more species, in addition to its five native species, espe-

Adult spiny mouse with her two week-old baby. The coat of the spiny mouse is made up of stiff bristles. A peculiarity of this rodent is that the tail is brittle and easily lost.

The European rabbit remained a pest in Europe and elsewhere until it was infected with the disease known as myxomatosis. Now scenes like this one are uncommon and the rabbit pest has been reduced, but at the price of introducing a loathsome disease.

Female muntjac in grass in England where it has been introduced and gone feral. France also has its feral muntjac. These small deer are often difficult to detect and their presence may go unsuspected until they start raiding crops.

cially if they increase in numbers. There is always the possibility that this can happen. For these introduced species and others detailed here, there is always the terrible lesson of the European rabbit.

At the time of the Roman Empire, the rabbit was confined to the Iberian peninsula. What happened to it is not known precisely. Some zoologists believe it was then a declining species, yet the Romans are believed to have used the ferret, the mongoose and, possibly, the genet to control it. If this last be true it must have been because the Romans cultivated the rabbit, keeping it in enclosures for the table. They also seem to have introduced it to other parts of western Europe, and in the twelfth century it was taken to Britain by the Normans. Certainly the rabbit flourished wherever it was taken, becoming in the end a pest, even a plague, although it was preyed upon by every carnivore and the larger birds of prey. Moreover, it was shot, trapped, poisoned and gassed by man, with little effect on its numbers. Finally, in 1953, in desperation, the disease known as myxomatosis was artificially introduced, causing a catastrophic drop in its numbers and increasing the yield of crops by about thirty per cent.

So far as mammals are concerned, man's greatest impact has usually been on those that can be used for food or clothing or as domestic beasts of burden. Two possible exceptions spring to mind: the dog and the cat. Yet even these, the universal pets of today, have in their long association with man had utilitarian values in addition.

If we are to judge by its present-day distribution, the bird that has entered most into human society is the domesticated pigeon, derived from the rock dove.

The native home of the rock dove is sea cliffs or inland cliffs, and today it is found wild right across the Mediterranean region, on the Ushant peninsula in western France, on cliffs around the coasts of Ireland and in the highlands of Scotland. The general opinion seems to be that Neolithic man probably first domesticated the pigeon. More certainly, it was domesticated by 5000 B.C. as can be shown by the discovery of figurines and other antiquities from the Middle East and the eastern Mediterranean region. Moreover, there seems little doubt that man first took the pigeon to his bosom as a symbol of love, fertility and peace. He later used it as a message-carrier, and also as food, the best evidence for which is in the numerous dovecotes or pigeon-houses scattered across Europe and south-west Asia, from the British Isles to Persia. Some of these dovecotes, either separate buildings associated with houses of the wealthy, or built into the houses or stables, are of great antiquity. They are, however, of all ages down to the eighteenth century. The largest of them have nesting places for 300 or more pairs of pigeons, representing a valuable source of fresh meat in days when butchers' shops were not as numerous as today, or were liable

PORTER/COLEMAN

SMITH/ARDEA

to be inaccessible to outlying patrons when foul weather intervened.

As wheeled transport increased and improved methods of distributing meat became available, the dovecote once again became ornamental, or fell into disuse. Its inmates became feral and tended to congregate in large towns where the human inhabitants soon took to feeding them. Houses, large public buildings, bridges and other architectural features provided excellent substitutes for cliff ledges for nesting. The feral pigeon flourished, even became a nuisance, if not a pest in places.

During the last 150 years the European starling has increased its range as well as its numbers. Another feature is that it has taken to roosting on buildings in large cities. As the afternoon draws to a close all the starlings in an area of countryside congregate and set off in huge flocks to their roosting places in clumps of trees or in the nearest town.

Above, left: The rock dove originally lived on cliffs. It was domesticated and large numbers were kept in dovecotes. Some of these escaped to give rise to feral or 'city' pigeons.

A cock pheasant in a woodland setting. Pheasants are now so familiar a part of the European fauna, and have been in the countryside so long, that they have become 'naturalized' and accepted as native.

GOOD/NHPA

One of the several species of birds that have adopted buildings for nesting is the summer visitor from southern Africa, the swallow, welcomed in Europe as the herald of summer. A remarkable feature is the fidelity with which a pair of swallows will return each year after a long absence and a journey of several thousand miles to the same nest-site in the same building.

Today it is cosmopolitan, in the tropics, in temperate latitudes, even living with man north of the Arctic Circle.

The pheasant just escaped being indigenous to Europe. Its native home is the province of Colchis, on the south side of the Caucasus, through which the river Phasis flows. It was taken to Greece but played no prominent part until it was taken to Italy, where it was kept in enclosures for fattening. Its eggs were also eaten. The Romans took it with them in their conquest of Europe. The ring-necked pheasant, with the white ring on the neck, is the product of crossing the original Colchis pheasant with Asiatic species.

For centuries the pheasant remained the game bird of the rich, bred and reared with care. In more recent times it went feral and is now established over most of Europe, as far north as Sweden. In some areas it is the most conspicuous, even characteristic, bird of the countryside, so much so that one almost loses sight of the fact that it is not a native.

In the same way we take for granted many birds that are familiar only because they are symbiotic with man. Swifts, swallows and house martins habitually nest in or on buildings but in exceptional cases may site their nests on coastal or inland cliffs, in caves or, for the swallow, on branches of trees. It can only be presumed from this that the natural nesting sites are mainly on cliffs. From this it would follow logically that man, by providing nesting sites with his buildings, must have been responsible for an enormous increase in the numbers of these birds. The process started so long ago, however, that there is no hope of proving this statistically.

Buildings are used, but less habitually, by many small birds for nesting, and this must be an important factor in the way they are distributed. It is noticeable, for example, that at least during the nesting season, there is a marked concentration of songbirds around areas of human habitations, such as villages or farmhouses, as compared with the open countryside. The wren, robin, the various tits, the spotted flycatcher, pied wagtail, sparrow, starling, even so large a bird as the jackdaw, make use of spaces, holes and crevices in buildings, small and large, for nesting sites. This combined with the growing human habit of putting up nesting boxes and bird-tables, and of putting out food for these birds, is having a cumulative effect on the numbers of what are now collectively grouped as "garden birds". More and more, birds are coming to these tables, with a noticeable increase in the great spotted woodpeckers, nuthatches and warblers, such as the blackcap, using bird-tables as accessory sources of food. There is even the suspicion that some blackcaps have given up their annual migration south because of this increased source of food.

One dividend from this growing human habit of "bird gardening" is that today, in some areas, it is almost impossible to grow soft fruits, peas and other produce of the kitchen garden without covering everything with nets.

Some of the worst of Europe's invaders are small and insignificant and of such long-standing that they tend to be accepted as native. In creating warm living quarters for himself, man has unwittingly created acceptable hostels for a number of insects, chiefly noxious. The bed bug, for example, probably came from the Middle East, although when or how is not known. It was certainly widespread in Germany by the eleventh century, and it was discovered in ports in the British Isles in the sixteenth century. During the next hundred years it had spread all over the country.

Cockroaches are by nature scavengers but because they settle where there is permanent heating this usually means bakeries and kitchens, where they are apt to get into the food. There are four species in Europe. One is the German cockroach *Blatella germanica*, but its actual place of origin is uncertain. The three others are more certainly international and include the American cockroach *Periplaneta americana,* the largest; the Oriental cockroach *Blatta orientalis*; and the Australian cockroach *Periplaneta australiae.* All three almost certainly reached Europe in ships' cargoes,

from North Africa via the Mediterranean ports and were then carried to towns all over Europe and Asia in early historical times, and later to the New World.

The house cricket that "sings" so monotonously in the bakehouse and on the hearth probably had a similar history to the cockroaches.

Ships have been responsible for other aliens, like the Australian acorn barnacle *Elminius modestus* that was carried on a ship's hull. It has become thoroughly established on rocks between tide-marks and in shallow water along Britain's coasts and tends to displace the indigenous acorn barnacles. A more troublesome ships' passenger was the Chinese river crab, 7 cm. across, also called the mitten crab from the "mitten" of hair-like bristles on each claw. This was first noticed in the River Aller, in Germany, in 1912. By 1935 it had spread to rivers across Europe from Flanders to Finland and south to Prague, and was so numerous that in the spring of 1935 no fewer than three and a half million were trapped near Bremen. These crabs burrow into banks of rivers and canals, undermining them. They interfere with important freshwater fisheries and also damage the green shoots of sprouting crops, although they are mainly scavengers. In China they are eaten as a delicacy. In Europe they have not graduated beyond being used for poultry and fertilizer.

Right: In several countries of Europe the white stork has long been welcomed as a bringer of good luck. There it has become the custom to erect some form of platform on the roof of the house to encourage the storks to nest.

Cockroaches are natural scavengers, but in their search for food become a nuisance in human habitations. They are not natives of Europe but are so widespread there and firmly established, they could almost be numbered among the indigenous fauna.

BEAMES/ARDEA

Bibliography

BELLAIRS, ANGUS: *The Life of Reptiles*, Vols. 1 and 2
Weidenfeld and Nicolson, London, 1969

BRINK, F H VAN DEN: *Zoogdierengids*
Elsevier, Amsterdam, 1955

BURTON, MAURICE: *Systematic Dictionary of Mammals of the World*
Museum Press, London, 1962

CLARK, W E LE GROS: *History of the Primates: an introduction to the study of fossil man*
British Museum (Natural History), London, 1949

CORBET, G B: *The Terrestrial Mammals of Western Europe*
Foulis, London, 1966

CURRY-LINDAHL, KAI: *Europe, a Natural History*
Hamish Hamilton, London and Random House, New York and Toronto, 1964

ELLERMAN, J R and MORRISON-SCOTT, T C S: *Check-list of Palaearctic and Indian Mammals*
British Museum (Natural History), London, 1951

GARMS, HARRY: *The Natural History of Europe*
Hamlyn, London, 1967. (Originally published as *Pflanzen und Tiere Europas*, George Westermann Verlag, Brunswick, 1962.)

GRAF, JAKOB: *Animal Life of Europe*
Warne, London and New York, 1968. (Originally published by Buchdruckerei Universal, Munich, 1961.)

HELLMICH, WALTER: *Reptiles and Amphibians of Europe*
Blandford, London, 1962. (Originally published as *Die Lurche und Kriechtiere Europas*, Carl Winter, Heidelberg, 1956.)

HIGGINS, L G and RILEY, N D: *A Field Guide to the Butterflies of Britain and Europe*
Collins, London, 1970

PETERSON, R, MOUNTFORT, G and HOLLOM, P A D: *A Field Guide to the Birds of Britain and Europe*
Collins, London, 1954

WHEELER, ALWYNE: *The Fishes of the British Isles and North West Europe*
Macmillan, London, 1969

ZEUNER, F E: *A History of Domesticated Animals*
Hutchinson, London, 1963

Glossary

Antirachitic vitamin Lack of this vitamin causes rickets.

Ascorbic vitamin Pure vitamin C, deficiency of which causes scurvy as well as dental disorders.

Aurignacian A culture, the remains of which are found at Cro-Magnon, in southern France.

Browser Animal that feeds on leaves and shoots of bushes and trees.

Caravanning Term used for family parties of shrews travelling in line, holding each other by the base of the tail.

Celt Ancient people of Western Europe, the Gauls and related ethnic groups.

Continental shelf Ledge of land fringing each continent above which the water is less than 183 m. deep. On the seaward side the edge of the shelf drops steeply in the continental slope to the ocean abysses.

Converter Name used to denote animals that by feeding on plant food provide animal protein for the animals that prey on them.

Deciduous Trees that shed their leaves in a short period of time (in the fall, or autumn).

Diurnal Active by day, opposite of nocturnal.

Feral A domesticated animal gone wild and breeding in the wild.

Food pyramid Diagrammatic representation of how at each step in a food chain the numbers decrease.

Glacial The Pleistocene epoch of the Quaternary period, when there were periodic glaciations.

Herbivorous Eating grass or herbs, in contrast to a **browser**.

Imago The last or adult stage in the life-history of an insect.

Insectivore A member of the order Insectivora (shrews, moles, hedgehogs, desmans) with teeth shaped for feeding on insects. (Insectivore dentition means the teeth, as in bats, are like those of the Insectivora.)

Interglacial A mild period separating two ice ages.

Limnology The study of fresh waters and their inhabitants.

Magdelenian The highest Paleolithic culture in western Europe named after La Madeleine near the station of Vézères in south-western France. Also called the reindeer people.

Merovingians Named from a line of Frankish kings reigning in Germany and Gaul, A.D. 500–A.D. 752.

Mesolithic Middle Stone Age, which ended about 10,000 years ago.

Mycorrhiza Association of fungal threads with roots of a higher plant.

Neanderthal man Race of primitive man having similar skulls to the one found at Neanderthal in Rhenish Prussia in 1857.

Neolithic New Stone Age whose people had learned to make polished stone implements.

Nymph Larval form in insects having an incomplete metamorphosis.

Omnivorous Eating plant and animal foods with little discrimination.

Ovipositor Tubular egg-laying organ seen especially in insects and a few fishes.

Paleolithic Old Stone Age, a people that used no more than stone chips or flakes.

Post-glacial Existing or occurring since the last ice age.

Phytophage Animal that feeds on plants. (The word has a wider connotation than **herbivore**.)

Predator Animal that preys on others.

Primeval Anything pertaining to the origins of the world or to ancient times generally.

Raptor One of the order Raptores (now no longer used), a bird of prey.

Solutrean Paleolithic culture named after characteristic flint implements first found in the Solutré Cave, in the department of Saône-et-Loire, France.

Sub-fossil Plant or animal remains dug out of the ground that were buried by natural agencies but too recently to be much altered in chemical or physical state.

Subspeciation The proliferation of subspecies.

Super-predator Animal at the apex of a **food pyramid**.

Ungulate A hoofed animal, name originally from the order Ungulata, which included all hoofed animals but is now obsolete.

Vole Mouse- or rat-like mammals distinguished from true mice and rats by having a blunt muzzle, small eyes and small ears almost hidden in the fur.

Index

Numbers in italics refer to illustrations.